TILSON

TILSON

POP TO PRESENT

ROYAL ACADEMY OF ARTS

First published on the occasion of
the exhibition 'Tilson: Pop to Present'

Royal Academy of Arts, London
14 March – 12 April 2002

Lenders to the Exhibition
Edinburgh, Scottish National Gallery of Modern Art
London, Arts Council Collection, Hayward Gallery
London, Tate
Minneapolis, Walker Art Center
Modena, Renata Pellerano
Verona, Collection Emilio Carpeggiani
Waddington Galleries Ltd
and those private collectors who wish to remain anonymous

The Royal Academy of Arts is grateful to Her Majesty's Government for its help in agreeing to indemnify the exhibition under the National Heritage Act 1980, and to the Museums and Galleries Commission for their help in arranging this indemnity.

EXHIBITIONS SECRETARY
Norman Rosenthal

EXHIBITION CURATOR
Isabel Carlisle

EXHIBITION ORGANISATION
Emeline Max
Marjorie Shiers

PHOTOGRAPHIC AND COPYRIGHT CO-ORDINATION
Andreja Brulc

CATALOGUE
Royal Academy Publications
David Breuer
Carola Krueger
Fiona McHardy
Peter Sawbridge
Nick Tite

Design: Maggi Smith
Colour origination: DawkinsColour Limited

Printed in Italy by Graphicom

British Library Cataloguing-in-Publication Data

A catalogue record for this book is available from the British Library

Distributed outside the United States and Canada by Thames & Hudson Ltd, London
ISBN 1-903973-11-2

Distributed in the United States and Canada by Harry N. Abrams, Inc., New York
ISBN 0-8109-6652-2

Limited edition
ISBN 1-903973-12-0

Acknowledgements
Joe Tilson would like to thank Alan Cristea, Giò Marconi, Giorgio Marconi, Reg and Pat Singh, and all at the Royal Academy.

Editor's Note
All measurements are given in centimetres, height before width before depth.

The extract from W. B. Yeats's 'Politics' is quoted with the permission of A. P. Watt Ltd on behalf of Michael B. Yeats. Copyright © 1940 by Georgie Yeats; copyright renewed 1968 by Bertha Georgie Yeats, Michael Butler Yeats, and Anne Yeats. In *The Collected Works of W. B. Yeats Volume 1, The Poems Revised*, edited by Richard J. Finneran. Reprinted with permission of Scribner, a Division of Simon & Schuster. The extract of Robert Duncan's 'At Home', Copyright the Literary Estate of Robert Duncan, is quoted with permission. The extract from Stephen Mitchell's translation of *The Ninth Elegy* by Rainer Maria Rilke, Copyright Stephen Mitchell, is reprinted with permission. Every effort has been made to trace the owners of copyright material, and any omissions are regretted.

Illustrations
Page 2: photograph of Joe Tilson in his studio by Aurelio Amendola. Page 7: detail of cat. 16. Page 51: detail of cat. 37.

Photographic Acknowledgements
All works of art are reproduced by kind permission of the owners. Specific acknowledgements for providing photographs are as follows: Edinburgh, Scottish National Gallery of Modern Art, cat. 7. Roy Fox, cats 2, 12, 16, 18, 19, 21, 22, 24, 26, 27, 29, 36, 37, 38. Howard Gimber, cats 14, 28, 30. London, courtesy the British Library Board, fig. 4. London, Prudence Cuming Associates Ltd, cats 25, 32; fig. 2. London © Tate/John Webb, cats 9, 11. Kiyoshi Togashi, fig. 3. Paolo Vandrasch, cat. 35. Copyright of all illustrated works by Joe Tilson © the artist. We are grateful to Joe Tilson for waiving copyright fees.

CONTENTS

PRESIDENT'S FOREWORD

Joe Tilson was finally elected to membership of the Royal Academy in 1985. He had first shown here in the now-legendary gallery of the 1975 Summer Exhibition which was selected by Peter Blake, still then an Associate Member. Peter included not only the 'Ruralists' but most of his 'Pop' friends and colleagues: Patrick Caulfield, R. B. Kitaj, David Hockney, Howard Hodgkin, Allen Jones and Tom Phillips, among others. Since then, nearly all of them have become Members, thereby infinitely enriching the Royal Academy and the way it is perceived in the outside world. Joe Tilson, at that time very much concerned in his art with ecological matters and mysteries of the countryside, showed his *Chthonic Box.* Made of wood and stone, it represented a small monument in an ongoing dialogue that Tilson has had through his art with the world around him: a considered flight from the city to the countryside.

Now, more than twenty-five years later, we are delighted to present a small but, because of Joe's detailed involvement, perfectly judged retrospective of an artist whose work is full of surprising complexities and intriguing poetic contradictions. Tilson here reveals his fascination with themes of childhood, such as building bricks and the meaning of primary colours, and equally strongly his interest in radical politics, popular culture, literature both ancient and modern, alchemy and philosophy. Those of us who have the privilege of knowing him realise how deeply he is engaged with books and with music across the widest range and how much they inform his art. Tilson is an artist of both city and country, of north and south; for many years now he has spent half the year in Italy, where his work is well-known and much appreciated, and half in England. Tilson lays these contradictions and choices before us in a beautifully crafted way that always says something about the cycles of life and our place within them.

A number of individuals have helped to organise and shape this exhibition, and, on behalf of the Royal Academy, I would like to thank them. Together with Norman Rosenthal, Isabel Carlisle has worked closely with the artist to make the exhibition happen smoothly. Mel Gooding has written a most stimulating essay for this catalogue that beautifully demonstrates the particular nature of Tilson's work. But, above all, we must thank Joe himself. He has taken the closest interest in every aspect of the show, choosing each work with Norman Foster's beautiful Sackler Wing of galleries very much in mind. This exhibition is a fascinating self-portrait of an artist who, over a long career with many phases and many interests in humanity and the natural world, has balanced everything into a most coherent life.

Professor Phillip King CBE
President, Royal Academy of Arts

FIRE
AIR
WATER
EARTH

'AN INCESSANT CREATION' NATURE AND METAPHOR IN JOE TILSON

MEL GOODING

1 TURNING PAGES, BOTH WAYS

'You must change your life'
Rainer Maria Rilke

Early in 1970 Joe Tilson said goodbye to the 1960s, a period in which he had enjoyed extraordinary success, with *Pages*, an exhibition and catalogue-publication of great originality.[1] The exhibition consisted of twenty mixed-media works, mostly screen and oil on canvas, mounted on wood-relief structures, and generically titled and numbered as *Pages 1–20*, each with a specific subtitle, together with a number of screenprints. With one significant exception, their imagery, drawing on newspaper photography and commercial lettering styles, referred to defining public events, media preoccupations and iconic personalities of the decade just ended: the civil rights movement, black power, Vietnam, fashion and famous female models, popular cinematic history, the 'underground press', Ho Chi Minh, Che Guevara, William Burroughs, Malcolm X, Martin Luther King. Their graphic style was of a kind that had been made possible by the screenprinting processes pioneered in this country by Chris Prater at Kelpra Press and taken up by many artists of the time, most notably Tilson's friends Richard Hamilton, Eduardo Paolozzi, Peter Blake and R. B. Kitaj, leading figures in the British Pop Art scene.

The great advantage of screenprinting for these artists was that it allowed the coexistence on a single, undifferentiated plane of visual materials drawn from quite diverse sources: a flat collage-montage which could combine photography, typographic and illustrative printed matter, old-fashioned and up-to-date advertising graphics, geometric and emblematic elements, and abstract free marks. This compendious capacity, which was being currently discovered and exploited, in their quite different ways, by Rauschenberg and Warhol in New York, was perfectly suited to the visual and verbal contrasts and accumulations, ironic, celebratory or simply poignant, that were the stock rhetorical devices of British Pop. Above all, allowing image-cropping, repetition and page layouts analogous to those of magazines and newspapers, and magnifying the dot matrix of press photography, it brought a stark mass-media immediacy into the art image.

In the mixed-media works and the screenprints that were brought together in *Pages*, Tilson took full advantage of the formal and thematic complexities afforded by the medium, but hinted at deeper themes than those that might have appeared to place his work within the ambit of media-conscious, politicised Pop. 'I've been trying to rub out the categories of both print as a minor medium and what you could do in a print,' he said to the art historian Pat Gilmour. 'Therefore, at one time, I made a list of the things you weren't meant to do, such as make it bulge, tear it up, cut it, make it out of materials that fell to pieces, make it out of plastic, and so on…'[2] In many of the wood-relief *Pages*, the photographic image is screenprinted onto small canvases, which were sewn by Tilson's wife Jos, herself an artist, into slightly bulging sacs. In each case these are mounted onto a wooden base within compartments separated by thin wooden struts, sometimes, as in *Page 8, Black Dwarf* (1969; cat. 17) and *Page 16, Ecology, Fire, Air, Water, Earth* (1969; cat. 16), with other compartments filled with wooden panels and relief elements. These structures resemble a printer's case, the divided tray in which type and spaces are held ready for use and which confers equality of regard to all of its contents. The analogy, with its implication that the artist is a journeyman, an artisan communicator, is to the technical array of signifying components necessary to printing, the democratic medium of a democratic message.

These box-like aspects give these works an emphatic objective presence, and suggest without irony the physical interchangeability of the component images, several of which recur across the series. These icons – Jean Shrimpton, Greta Garbo, Claude Lévi-Strauss,

Herbert Marcuse and Martin Luther King among them – represent in their being, in their action or thought or both, the passional life, which includes the life of the mind, freed from the constraints of determinist, mechanistic or repressive politics. This temporal politics is that to which Yeats refers in 'Politics', some of whose verses are reproduced in *Page 19, He, She & It* (1969–70; cat. 18), and whose epigraph is from Thomas Mann: 'In our time the destiny of man presents its meaning in political terms.' The poem, written in 1938 or 1939, the poet's own last year, towards the end of 'a low dishonest decade' dominated by political betrayals and war, repudiates this reductive view of a politicised humanity:

> 'How can I, that girl standing there
> My attention fix
> On Roman or on Russian
> Or on Spanish politics?'

Despite a laconic acknowledgement that what politicians say may be true 'of war and war's alarms', the speaker declares his true allegiance:

> 'But O that I were young again
> And held her in my arms!'[3]

The soft, filled pillows of the image-supports take on entirely appropriate allusive properties in the light of the poem (whose last lines paraphrase an ancient anonymous verse, *Westron Winde*: 'Christ! if my love were in my arms/And I in my bed again').

Pages, in its presentation of discrete works and integral catalogue as a coherent whole, was informed by a crucial poetic idea that gave the exhibition a significance that went beyond its elegiac and subtle renunciation of the conventional adversarial politics of the late 1960s. It was the central idea of *symboliste* poetics: Mallarmé's 'Tout, au monde, existe pour aboutir à un livre', 'Everything in the world exists to end up in a book.' The Book was conceived by the great French poet as a 'spiritual instrument' whose purpose was to effect the alchemical transformation of the contingent objects and events of the material world into an encoded image, a distillation, a timeless transcendence of the immediate natural, cultural and political moment. In essence, Mallarmé's great remark is a restatement of the ancient and recurring notion of the poet as Orphic interpreter: the work of the creative imagination is to read the world and interpret it to ourselves. Extending this idea to all the arts reveals

Fig. 1 TRANSPARENCY, THE FIVE SENSES: SIGHT, 1969
Screenprinted and vacuum-formed acrylic sheet, 147.5 × 147.5 × 4 cm.
Ludwig Múzeum, Budapest

a beautiful paradox: things become words, are defined in words and signs; abstract words and ideas are replaced by images of things. It is a poetics of metaphor in which the movement of the dance, the reverberating sound of music, poetic images of objects and events rather than the abstractions of discursive thought, and the objects or actions of the visual artist become carriers of meanings that cannot be articulated in discursive and rational language, and which find their way into the mind through the senses of the body.

Tilson, who was working in 1969 and 1970 with an acute sense of the multifarious failures of the hopes of 1968, was seeking a mode of artistic expression that would connect with his sense of a perennial human world in which sensory pleasure and aesthetic joy in nature, the realities of Eros and Dionysus, had primacy over those values – identified by Marcuse with Prometheus – of control and command, of 'toil, productivity and progress through repression'.[4] In many of his earlier works, then, as now, celebrated as classics of Pop Art, Tilson had projected the significance of the human subject whose senses are the key to the world. Works such as *Vox Box* (cat. 11) and *Nine Elements* (cat. 7), both of 1963, and *Look!* (1964; cat. 10) are early workings of a theme that finds its definitive Pop expression in the *Transparency* series of 1969 (see fig. 1), represented

Fig. 2 EARTHEARTHEARTH, 1974. Oak, 183 × 208 × 5 cm. Private collection

here by the marvellous *Transparency, The Five Senses: Taste* (cat. 9), in which the generic title refers not only to the blown-up Ektachrome, but to the necessity of direct and unmediated sensation: 'If the doors of perception were cleansed everything would appear to man as it is, infinite.'

Page 16, Ecology, Fire, Air, Water, Earth (1969; cat. 16) is both a valedictory celebration and a portent of things to come. It is a kind of pantheon, in which the elements of a truly human ecology include not only those of the ancient quartet from which the natural environment is created, but also the work and spirit of those who have argued and fought for a kinder accommodation for humankind on the earth. (Tilson would have been aware of the primary Greek root of ecology: *oikos* = house.) Hence the predominance in the frame of political and (in the broadest sense) anthropological thinkers whose vision had informed the political ethics of the decade. An honoured place is found for the Caduveo Indian girl from the Mato Grosso, the photograph of whose painted face by Lévi-Strauss was reproduced in *Tristes Tropiques*, his visionary elegy for an aboriginal world on the wane.[5] Below the array of faces are six box-compartments of building blocks arranged into the pyramids and ziggurats familiar from many of Tilson's relief works of the 1960s. Here, as in those earlier works, they represent the constructive impulse that finds its first expression in play, and a technology that has spiritual and mystical dimensions. In the early 1970s, as he gathered materials for his *Alchera* manifesto, Tilson was to make a number of simple wooden block constructions in basic configurations (fig. 2).

Wooden blocks like these were first introduced by Friedrich Froebel, the inventor of the kindergarten, to bring delight as they structure thinking and learning through active play and experiment (fig. 3). Through the thought and practice of many of its greatest protagonists who attended kindergarten in their formative years (they include Mondrian, Klee, Kandinsky, Frank Lloyd Wright and Le Corbusier), the Froebelian kindergarten and its philosophy had a profound influence on modernism in art and architecture. In his revelatory book on the subject, Norman Brosterman describes the rich possibilities of meaning to be found in the use of building blocks in terms that apply closely to their signifying purposes in a work such as *Page 16, Ecology*, in earlier works, such as *A–Z Box of Friends and Family* (1963; cat. 3) and *Astronaut Puzzle* (1963; cat. 5), and in the *Alchera* works of the following decade: '[their open-ended nature] provides opportunities for

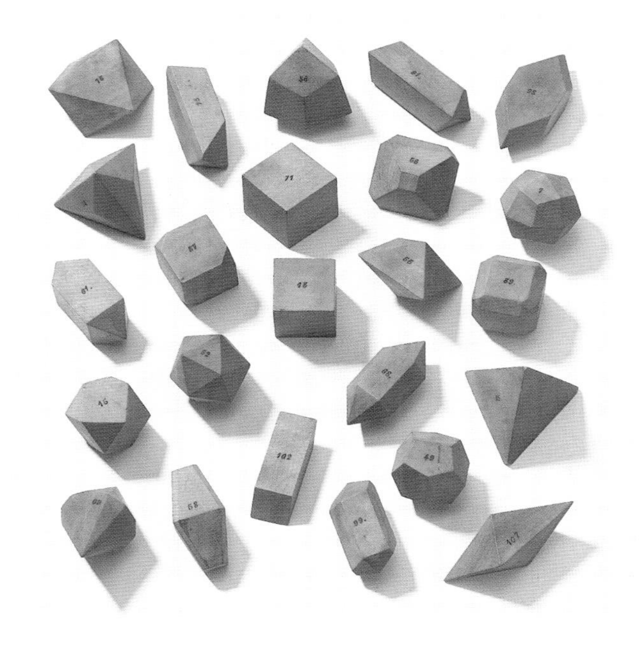

Fig. 3 FRIEDRICH FROEBEL
Crystals, c. 1900

instruction in social studies – in mapping, the layout of cities, and people's work; socialisation – in cooperation, cleanup, respect for others, and self-confidence; art and architecture – in pattern, balance, symmetry, and construction; language – in function, story-telling, planning and conceptual exchange; science – in gravity, weight, trial and error, and inductive thinking; and mathematics – in geometry, number, measurement, classification, fractions, and much more.'[6]

It was not only building blocks that Froebel introduced into the education of infants: there was the garden itself, with independent and communal plots for the growing of flowers and vegetables, and, among other materials of his system (Froebel called them the 'gifts'), a boxed set of wooden Sphere, Cylinder and Cube, boxed marquetry kits, paper kits for grid and interlock pattern-making, and clay for modelling. These were to be used in the disciplined exploration of the 'three realms' of a unified knowledge: of the forms of nature (life), the forms of knowledge (science) and the forms of beauty (art). Without his being aware of it, Tilson's creative technologies have constituted an extraordinary recapitulation of the Froebelian principles of mental and spiritual construction, most particularly in their emphasis upon the dialectics of complexity and simplicity, on the connectivity between all things, and on the dynamic unity of the manifold in phenomenological experience. Significantly, his involvement with the development of his own children, and his sense of art as the product of a collaborative community, led Tilson into the games-like box and cumulative relief forms that were his distinctive contribution to Pop. They were signalled most remarkably, early in the 1960s, by the marquetry screen-like works *For Jake and Anna* (1961; cat. 2) and *For Jos January 1st* (1963), both of which have a heraldic butterfly-wing symmetry, and by *A–Z Box of Friends and Family*, a container of gifts in celebration of artistic friendship.

2 COUNTRY MATTERS: GRAPE, GRAIN AND OLIVE; BIRDS, GODS AND BUTTERFLIES

> 'When silence
> Blooms in the house, all the paraphernalia of our existence
> Shed the twitterings of value, and reappear as heraldic devices'
> Robert Duncan[7]

Tilson has always loved the idea of order, of things in order, the right order; not of course that other kind of Order, with a capital O, against which he has pitted himself in his art from the beginning. The order he loves is that of the library, of the carpenter's workshop or the well-organised studio, of the printer's type-case, where things are in their proper place, their names known, waiting for their usefulness to be manifest in thinking, doing and making; or the order of the house and habitat, of the farmer's field, the vineyard and the grove, the barn and the yard. His workbooks, numbered and dated, are identified by accounts-book labels, horizontal rectangles and octagons with a blue outline, their lettering stencilled and businesslike. They are for taking account of things, keeping accounts of things and events, taking things into account. Keeping them is a habit necessary to the discovery of the order of art, that 'idea of order' which for Wallace Stevens was the key to a reading of the world as 'a supreme fiction', his version of Mallarmé's 'Book'. 'There is no "world" out there to be copied into art,' Tilson wrote in a workbook, close to an inscription of Mallarmé's statement, 'Art itself creates what we call the world.'

In July 1970, shortly after the showing of *Pages*, Tilson went to Hanover, the home city of Kurt Schwitters, where, on encountering the Easter Firewheel in the Historisches Museum, he experienced the epiphany 'WOOD AND FIRE'. The significance of the moment and its consequences for Tilson's art from that time on are revealed, though not in discursive terms, in *Alchera*, his great encyclopaedic manifesto of 1976–77, in which he documented the works of the early 1970s in a *mélange* of statements, quotations, fragments of text, drawings, charts and photographs that reflected a mind immersed in poetry and myth, philosophy ancient and modern, cultural history and anthropology. The body of creative works gathered under the order of *Alcherae*, to use the conceit of a naturalist's classification, may be said to have originated in the exceptional *Page 1, Penelope* (1969; fig. 4), the first work in the 1970 exhibition. In the catalogue it is faced by the last few lines of Joyce's *Ulysses*, ending in the word 'Yes', and by a quotation of a letter from Joyce on the significance of the final – Penelope/Molly Bloom – episode: 'Penelope is the *clou* of the book.' There is also Joyce's response to an interviewer's question: 'Yes, you're right. The book must end with yes, it must end with the most positive word in the human language.'

In 1970 'all the paraphernalia' of Tilson's 1960s, the temporal imagery of an historical era, was left behind, its significance neither denied nor repudiated. In *Page 1* a new phase of work was begun with the affirmative repetition, in 169 compartments of a perfectly square case, of Joyce's 'most positive word' in woodblock lettering: the word presented as an object, infinitely repeatable in every direction, north, south, west, east, up and down and side to side; an image-mantra, in which the phonemic structure, the word-sound, is transformed into an abstract visual object-sign. Poetry and myth (in its broadest interpretation) were central to this new body of work, and poetry was integral to its earliest conception. Confronted by the Firewheel, Tilson had thought of Rilke's lines from *The Ninth Elegy*, and they provided him with a key to the kind of artist he would be from this time on:

> 'For when the traveller returns from the mountain-slopes
> into the valley,
> he brings, not a handful of earth, unsayable to others, but instead
> some word he has gained, some pure word, the yellow and
> blue gentian. Perhaps we are *here* in order to say: house
> bridge, fountain, gate, pitcher, fruit tree, window –
> at most: column, tower... But to *say* them, you must understand,
> oh, to say them *more* intensely than the Things themselves
> ever dreamed of existing.'[8]

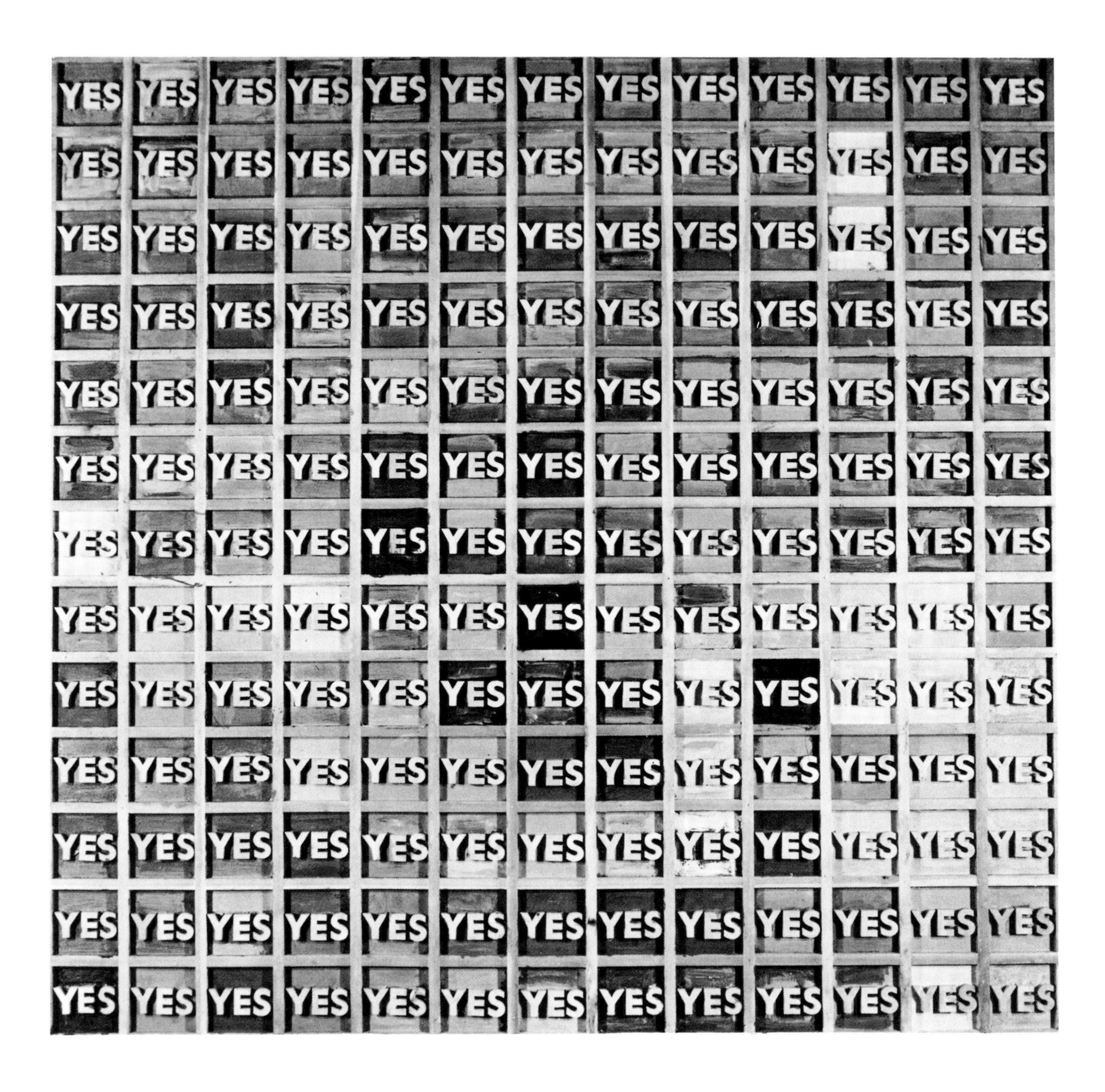

Fig. 4 PAGE 1, PENELOPE, 1969. Oil on wood relief, 199.5 × 199.5 cm. The British Library, London

Among the first works that Tilson made in the new manner, in 1971, were *Ladders* (see cat. 25), into whose rungs were branded words drawn from poems by Dante, Rilke and Schwitters. In the case of Schwitters (whose own female muse figure is also a Bloom: Anna Blume, 'beloved of my twenty-seven senses'), Tilson burned into the ladder steps the contracted and compressed words of a near-nonsense love poem, *He, She & It*, whose title he had used for two of the 1969–70 *Pages* that are devoted to a celebration of the female principle (cat. 18). From Rilke he took the list of object-words; from Dante those words that begin with the final letter of the alphabet, that most objective letter, 'z'. Such 'pure words', together with words of Tilson's own, said '*more* intensely than the Things themselves ever dreamed of existing', became integral to the objects he made. Ladders, like stacks and stakes, grid compartments and chequerboards, all of which devices Tilson now used in his work, allow for the disposition of words and objects (and word-objects) in non-hierarchical configurations that suggest possibilities of infinity. To those generic forms he added others: the egg, the box, the sphere and the cube, the triangle, the circle entire, or with twofold or fourfold division, and the labyrinth (fig. 5). Each is satisfying in its formal completeness, each replete with signifying and symbolic potential. Each work belongs, with

Fig. 5 Retrospective at the Museum Boijmans van Beuningen, Rotterdam, 1971

a perfect simplicity, to a world in which earth, water, air and fire are everyday realities. Each is part of the Orphic interpretation; each carries a mythic burden. 'There is no single "true" version of which all the others are but copies or distortions,' wrote Lévi-Strauss in *Structural Anthropology*,[9] in a passage of which Tilson was well aware: 'Every version belongs to the myth.'

Working with wood, rope, straw and other natural materials, Tilson was able now to give full rein to his love of the ordered technologies of carpentry and joinery, the journeyman skills he had learned as a young man at the Brixton School of Building long before he had gone to art school. In 1973 he removed from London with his family to a rambling old house, the Old Rectory at Christian Malford in Wiltshire, and here, and at Casa Cardeto, his farmhouse near Cortona in Tuscany, he was able to work away from the distractions of the city. He had found the garden, a ground to cultivate, and a place to work at an art that consciously, and conscientiously, removed itself from the immediate cultural and political moment, and located itself within the time of the mythic, the perennial time of the diurnal and seasonal cycle. 'These country places of the Tilsons', wrote the poet Jonathan Williams in *Alchera*, '[became] granaries filled by a new husbandry…Joe Tilson's is a redolent mind at work.'[10]

Fig. 6 ELEUSIS II, 1991–92. Oil on canvas on wood relief, 216.5 × 217 cm. Private collection

It is a mind that returns insistently and ineluctably to the elemental and elementary oppositions that make the simple and powerful *Mnemonic Device* (1973; cat. 20) so effective a summation of the ideas and experience of the *Alchera* period, though Tilson continued to work in that spirit and style for some years.

By the end of the 1970s there was a growing insistence in works in various media on thematic material and visual and verbal reference to the myths of ancient Greece. This reflected a deepening feeling for the Mediterranean, and its mythologies, in which the poetic and the natural, word, image and object (Rilke's '[things that] we are *here* in order to say'), are fused. In the Italy and Greece of Tilson's imaginings, the primal cycles were registered in the tangible realities of the agricultural year, in the cyclic field work, in the felt relation of wine to vine, oil to olive, cheese to goat, of good and necessary things to their sources in nature. The mythic was vividly ever-present, assimilated to the quotidian. Tilson's paintings and votive screens of the 1980s and early 1990s (fig. 6) took on, with a characteristic literal simplicity, the character of offerings and celebrations in which signs for things – sun and moon, sapling, leaf and branch, pomegranate, seed and raisin, the jar for water, wine or oil – are joined by the hand and eye of human apprehension, spiral and labyrinths symbolic of hidden energies and mysteries, and the lettered names of the gods.

In works such as the *Moon* and *Sun Signatures* of 1985 (cats 33 and 34), Tilson returned to painting by hand, bringing brilliant colour back into his art, and with Jos Tilson, turned to ceramics, the most ancient and elemental of the arts. In all his work from this time on, Tilson has given expression to a directly sensuous relation to the material world of nature and agriculture. His response to the landscape is shaped by a sense of being there as himself a creator of its forms: the poet-artist joins the peasant-farmer in the shaping of reality. Both are makers of definitions; both are technologists in the sense of the word that derives from the ancient Greek: skilful, artful practitioners. And both are, in Mircea Eliade's fine phrase, 'technicians of the sacred', respecting and revering the earth as the ground of being. This human, and humane, presence in the country requires the poetry of word and of image for the maintenance of its vitality in the consciousness of those who live in the culture of cities. '*Here*', in Rilke's words, 'is the time for the *sayable*, *here* is its homeland.'

Liknon 3 (1987; cat. 32) and *The Flaying of Marsyas C* (1989; cat. 31) take constructive forms that relate back to Tilson's earlier compartmentalising reliefs, but their configurations suggest a spiral dynamic rather than the lateral and vertical arrangement of the grid. Their facture is freely expressive, handmade, hand-lettered. The artist's hand is present in the work; the message, that we must maintain connection, stay in touch, with primal realities, is implicit in the medium. They deny the window frame of Western landscape painting, the controlling eye and single vision of perspective: they are emblematic and evocative rather than descriptive or discursive. The *Crete Senesi* of the early 1990s (cats 35–38) share this quality, as do the spectacular *Conjunctions* (cats 39–43) of more recent years. They are objects, not pictures. They rejoice in the free forms and brilliant colours of nature even as they transform them into shape and pattern, finding in the symmetries of natural forms an intimation of the numinous.

To conceive of the world as a book is to see reality in the light of the sign, and to express it in metaphor. Wallace Stevens, another of the great modernist poets in whose light Tilson works, quotes another writer on the nature of the printing press, the technology that had provided Tilson with potent metaphors in much of his work before the turning point of 1969–70: 'The business of the press is to furnish an indefinite public with a potentially indefinite number of identical texts.' In terms that are immediately relevant to our experience of Tilson's late paintings and prints, Stevens replies: 'Nature is not mechanical to that extent for all its mornings and evenings…for all its waves, or its leaves, or its hands. Its prodigy is not identity but resemblance and its universe of reproduction is not an assembly line but an incessant creation. Because this is so in nature, it is so in metaphor.'[11]

NOTES AND SOURCES

1. *Pages*, exh. cat., Marlborough Fine Art, London, March – April 1970.
2. For Tilson's conversation with Pat Gilmour, see Tate Archive, 4 November 1975.
3. W. B. Yeats, 'Politics', from 'Last Poems: 1936–39', in *The Collected Poems of W. B. Yeats*, London, 1963.
4. Tilson quotes this passage from Hubert Marcuse's *Eros and Civilisation* in *Pages*.
5. Claude Lévi-Strauss's *Tristes Tropiques*, Paris, 1955, was first published in England as *A World on the Wane*, London, 1961.
6. Norman Brosterman, *Inventing Kindergarten*, New York, 1997.
7. Robert Duncan, 'At Home', in *Derivations: Selected Poems, 1950–56*, London, 1968.
8. Rilke is quoted from the translation by Stephen Mitchell (Picador Classics, London, 1987).
9. *Structural Anthropology* was published in English in New York and London in 1963.
10. *Alchera*, 1970–76, was published by La Nuova Foglia Editrice, Pollenza-Macerata.
11. Wallace Stevens's 'Three Academic Pieces' (he is quoted from the first) were published in *The Necessary Angel*, London, 1960.

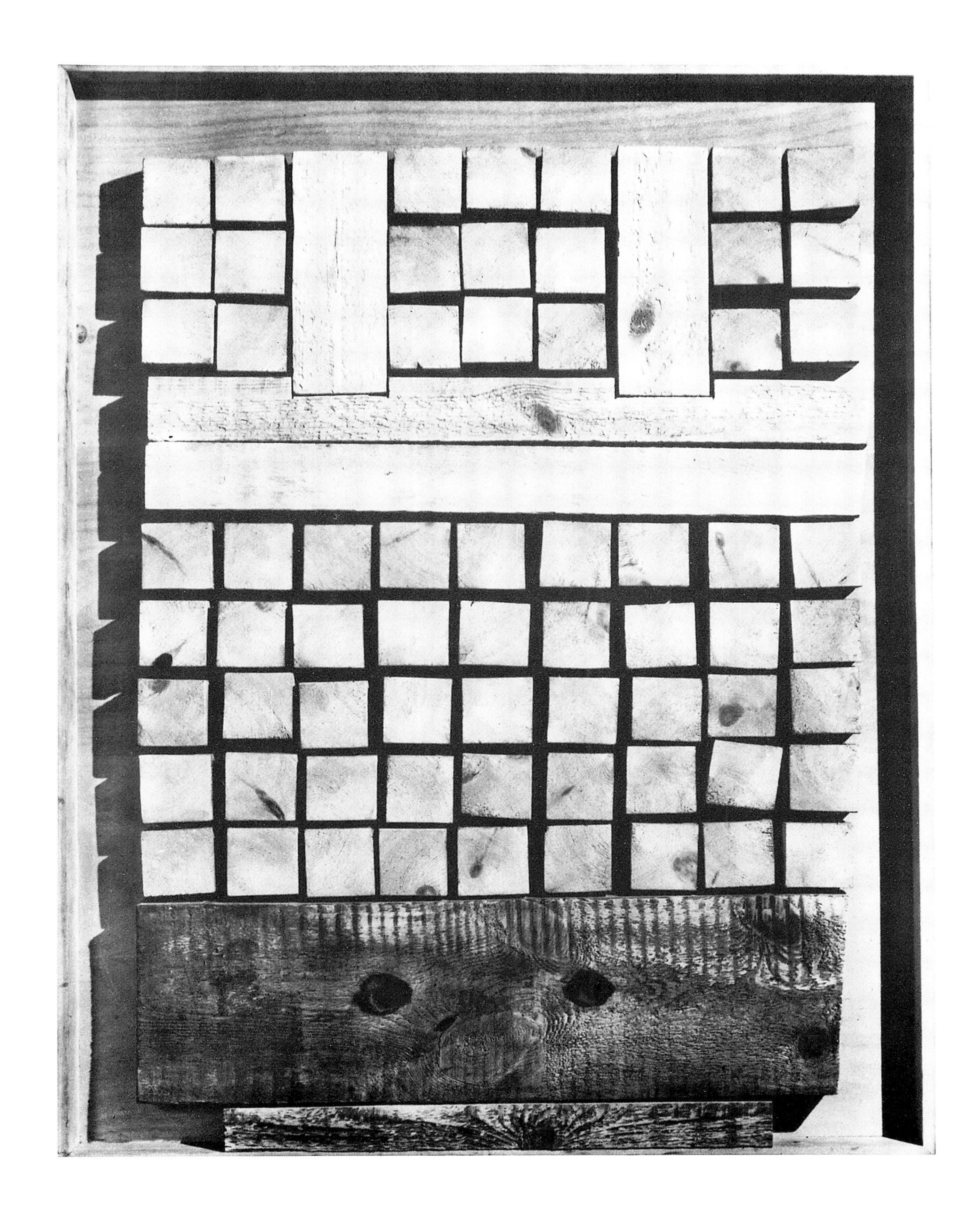

1 WOOD RELIEF NO. 17, 1961. Wood, 125 × 95 × 8 cm. Tate. Purchased 1962

2 FOR JAKE AND ANNA, 1961. Oil on wood relief, 96.5 × 127 cm. Private collection

3 A–Z BOX OF FRIENDS AND FAMILY, 1963. Mixed media, 233 × 152 cm. Private collection

4 GEOMETRY? 3, 1964. Oil and acrylic on wood relief, 188 × 188 cm. Private collection

5 ASTRONAUT PUZZLE, 1963. Oil on wood relief, 132 × 102 × 8 cm. Collection Emilio Carpeggiani, Verona

6 KEY BOX, 1963. Oil on wood relief, 182 × 144 × 27 cm. Private collection, Milan

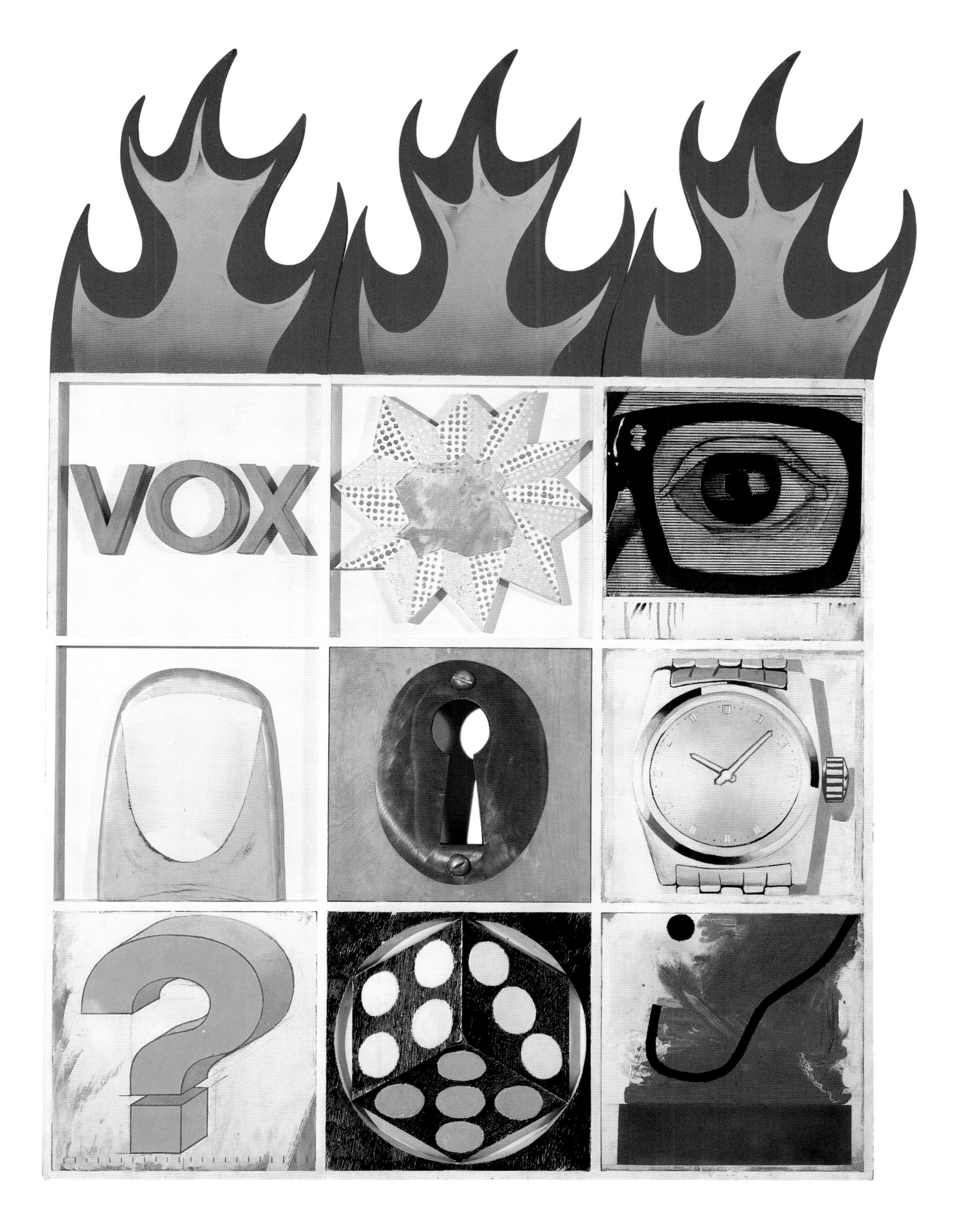

7 NINE ELEMENTS, 1963. Kandy, pearl and acrylic on wood relief, 259 × 183 cm.
Scottish National Gallery of Modern Art, Edinburgh. Purchased 1983

8 21ST, 1963. Oil on canvas and board, 170 × 121 × 3 cm. Renata Pellerano, Modena

9 TRANSPARENCY, THE FIVE SENSES: TASTE, 1969. Screenprinted and vacuum-formed acrylic sheet, 147.5 × 147.5 cm.
Tate. Presented by Marlborough Graphics through the Institute of Contemporary Prints, 1970

10 LOOK!, 1964. Oil, acrylic on wood relief, 186.69 × 195.58 × 7.62 cm. Collection Walker Art Center, Minneapolis Art Center Acquisition Fund, 1966

11 VOX BOX, 1963. Oil on wood relief, 153 × 122 cm. Tate. Purchased 1976

12 SKY, GREEK CROSS AND DODECAGON, 1967. Tri-chromatic screen and polyurethane on wood relief, 122 × 244 × 10 cm. Private collection

13 ZIKKURAT 7, 1967. Oil and acrylic on wood relief, 187 × 295 × 14 cm. Arts Council Collection, Hayward Gallery, London

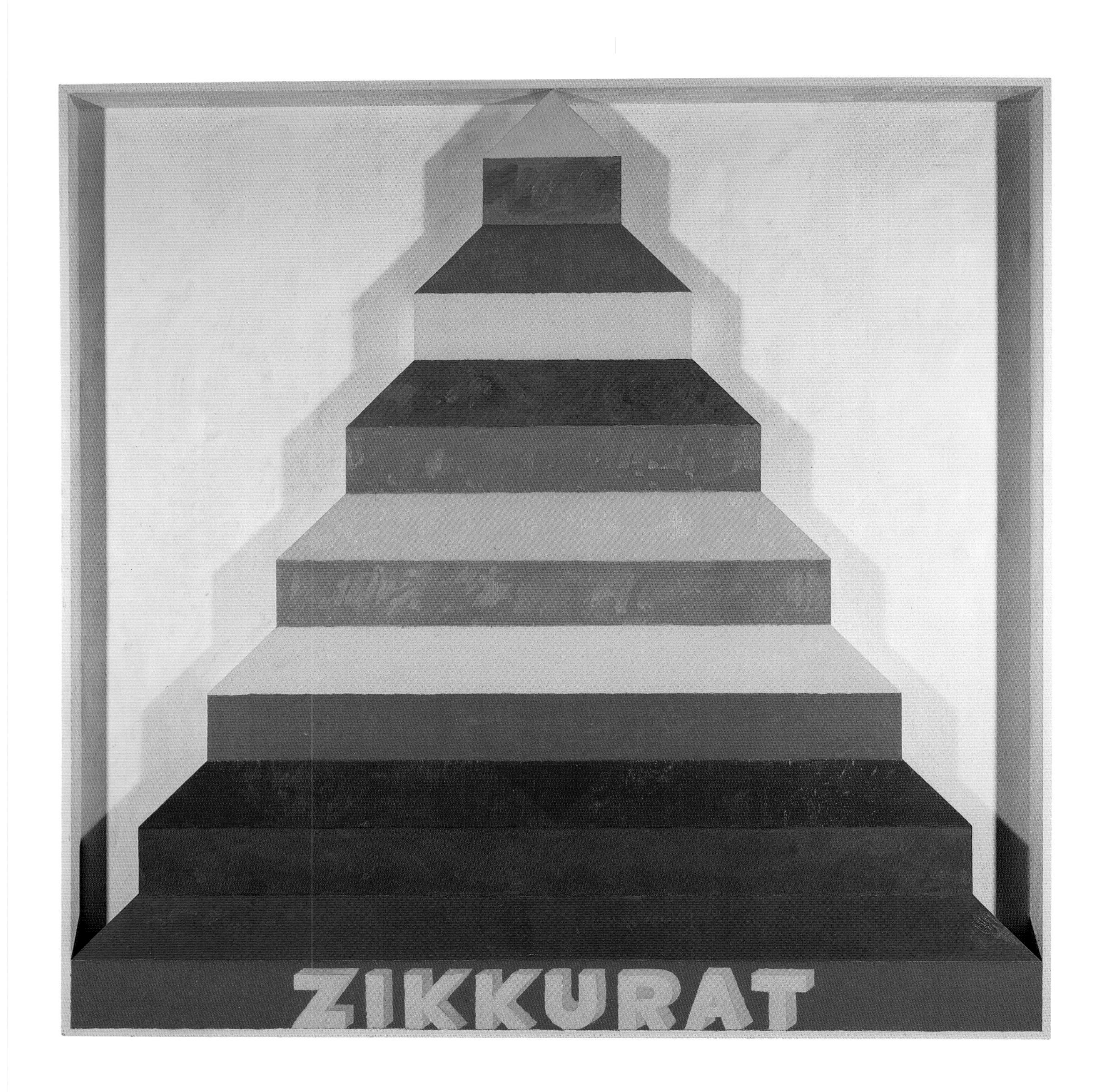

14 ZIKKURAT 3, 1967. Oil and acrylic on wood relief, 216 × 216 cm. Private collection

15 ZIKKURAT 9, 1967. Oil and acrylic on wood relief, 214 × 214 × 14 cm. Private collection

 PAGE 16, ECOLOGY, FIRE, AIR, WATER, EARTH, 1969. Screen and oil on canvas on wood relief, 169 × 169 cm. Private collection

17 PAGE 8, BLACK DWARF, 1969. Screen on canvas on wood relief, 187 × 126 cm. Private collection

 PAGE 19, HE, SHE & IT, 1969–70. Screen and oil on canvas on wood relief, 187 × 126 cm. Private collection

19 PAGE 18, MUHAMMAD SPEAKS, 1969–70. Screen and oil on canvas on wood relief, 187 × 126 cm. Private collection

ALCHERA (1970-73)

dedicated to Epos & Ὀρφεύς & other juices rising intofruit..

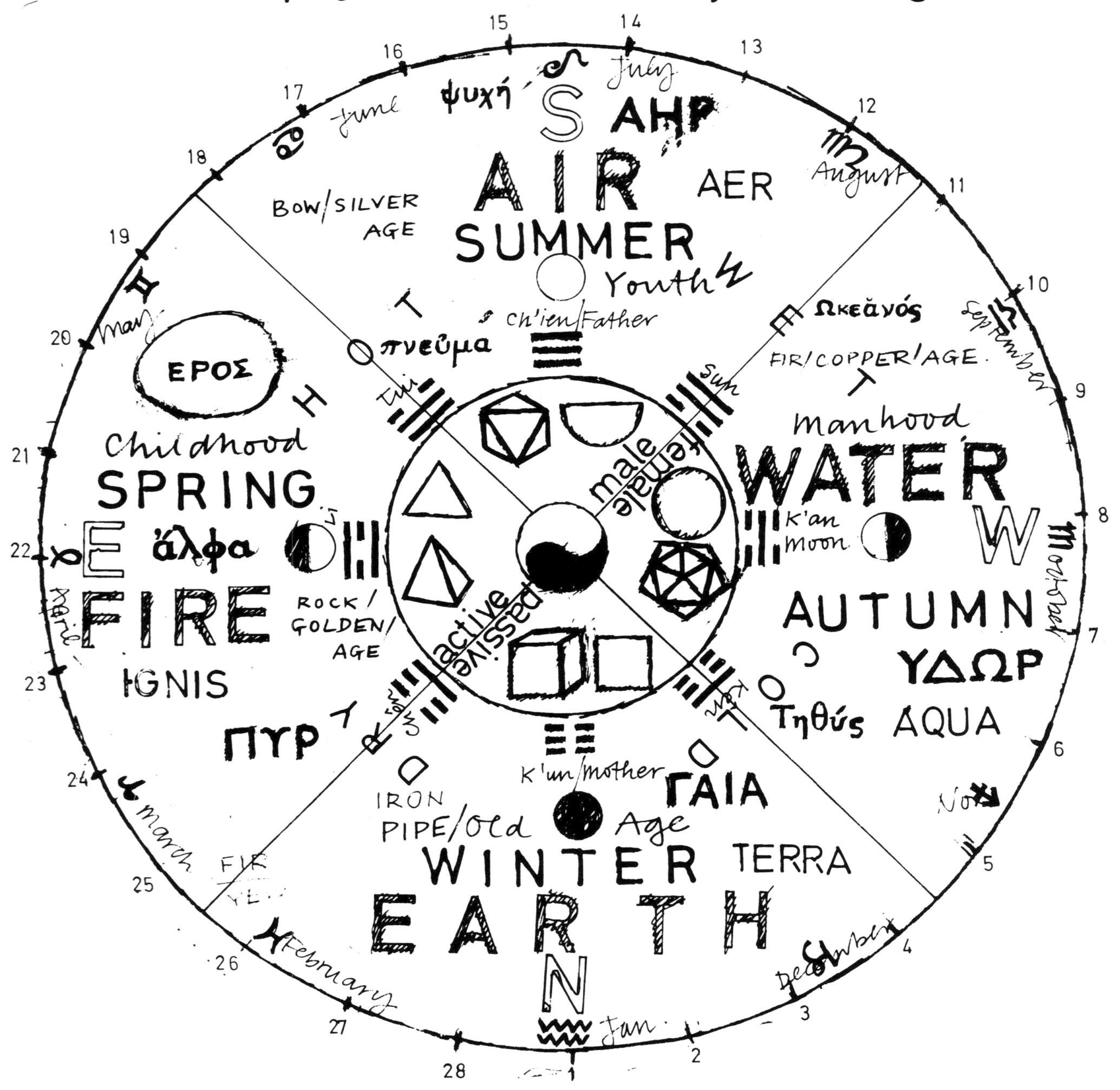

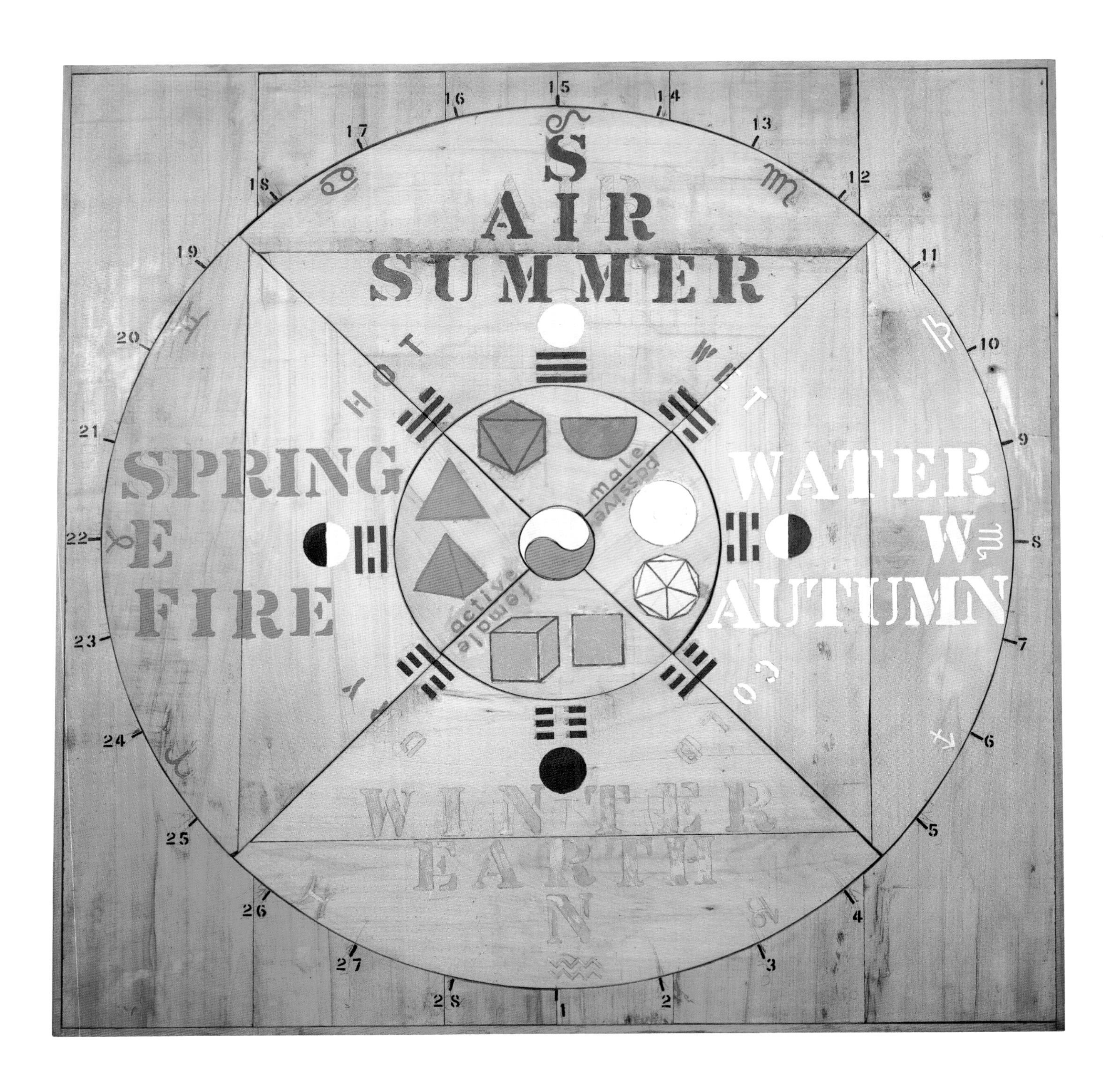

20 MNEMONIC DEVICE, 1973. Oil on wood panel, 211 × 211 cm. Private collection

1

Chi con ciglia inarcate
E labbra strette
Non va per questo loco
Le famose del Mondo
Moli sette

MANCO
AMMIRA

He who fails to.pass through
this place with eyes wide open
lips pressed shut
will fail to admire
the seven wonderful structures
of the world

(On the pedestal of a Sphinx at Bomarzo)

NOTES FOR ALCHERA

dedicated to EROS and ORPHEUS, and to other juices rising into fruit.
As the Big Fire Source said:

These Days
Whatever you have to say, leave
the roots on, let them
dangle
And the dirt
just to make clear
where they came from.

ALCHERA: DREAMTIME
IN ILLO TEMPORE
AB ORIGINE
FRUMSCEAFT: GENESIS: FIRST SHAPES
(Caedmons Hymn)

As a change from the usual pinch of salt, I would ask you with Picabia: "Pendant que vous lirez ces lignes, sucez je vous prie le jus d'une cerise". As these notes are forced by the linear process of writing to impose an order on my work that leaves out the actual experience of the work - they are essentially false. And can only be read as clues to an approach to the objects which contain their own mute truth. I think of these notes rather like an Ordnance survey map of a cloud of steam.

ALCHERA is the Dreamtime of Australian Magic

The dream is a real objective experience in which time and space are no longer obstacles, and in which information of great importance is gained by the dreamer. The information may refer to the sky world of the Aranda in which time and space are no longer obstacles, and so a person's totem may link him to that period and give him a share in it.... to those with eyes to see; rocks and trees, rivers and hills, are 'Dreamings', marking the deeds of the mythical heroes and the places where the spirits of men and animals dwell.... a man's dreaming is his share in the myths or rites of the traditions of the old or eternal dream time.

2

My involvement dates back from July 1970 when I went to Germany to discuss a possible project for 'Strassenkunst Hanover' and saw the Easter Fire Wheel in the Historiches Museum there:- WOOD AND FIRE
I thought of letters burnt into wood with brands like those used for branding cattle and of wooden objects slowly covered with Lichens, Moss, Ivy, Vines or small-leaved plants - of objects that had words on them that slowly disappeared.
I thought of the poen of Rilke:

Are we, perhaps, here just for saying: House, Bridge, Well,
Gate, Jug, Fruit-tree, Window - possibly Pillar, Tower?....
but for saying, remember, oh, for such saying as never
the things themselves hoped so intensely to be.

I started work on a series of objects - a window, a large wood ziggurat, huge wooden biscuits with one word in the centre, poems on wood stakes, a giant wooden egg, and a coloured ladder with a poem by Kurt Schwitters on it:

Er Sie Es
unt
hund
Tak
Pack
Karakte
Duumdu
dirindir
Gott Gnadetu
leben
laufen
streben
vergeben
schenken
dirindir
tak
pack
duumdu
du

To be made in modest materials - and related to grass, flowers, leaves, trees, bushes, the river, the Beginenturm, the Bridge, children passing, old people sitting on the benches by the river opposite the Hohen Ufer.
Two of these objects were to stand together on the grass by the river opposite the Beginenturm, attached to concrete bases completely hidden with grass grown up to them. The project was not accepted by Hanover, nor my other project, that of turning off all the letters of the neon signs on all the COMMERZ UND PRIVATBANK's except the word MERZ, in honour of Schwitters!
But the idea of the burn brand letters and the egg were still with me.

My wife Jos had recently been publishing a periodical for contracts between artists, called CATALYST, and so was exchanging with Steve Baer of 'Dome Cookbook' and the Shuttleworths of Mother Earth News. Laura Besserman was sending us the first

21 FIRE BOX and ALCHERINGA FIRE BOX, 1971–72
Wood boxes with wood sculpture, straw and photographs,
30.5 × 30.5 × 30.5 cm; 23 × 30.5 × 30.5 cm. Private collection

22 AIR BOX and ALCHERINGA AIR BOX, 1971–72
Wood boxes with sculpture, feathers and photographs,
30.5 × 30.5 × 30.5 cm; 23 × 30.5 × 30.5 cm. Private collection

3

Whole Earth Catalogs - all this exchange of information and the people we contacted plus our recent involvement with Artists Information Registry, the St. Katherine's dock scheme for artists' studios, and FACOP - a group of artists attacking the Establishment; all this led us to change our views completely on our life. It finally led us to leave London, and now we spend the summer months at a farm in Italy, and the rest of the year in Wiltshire - to become, like Wordsworth:

> If not a Settler on the soil, at least
> To drink wild water, and to pluck green herbs,
> And gather fruits fresh from their native bough.

But the first steps for me in 1970 and 1971 were to take the idea of using fire in my work and to start a series of ladders and eggs and to begin the project of the Four Elements - FIRE, AIR, WATER and EARTH. Not in any anti scientific spirit, but because they are, and alway will be, the four elements of imaginative experience - unlike Technetium, Einseinium, Hafnium, Ytterbium, or Yttrium to mention but a few of the 103 elements known to science!

Having divided two pages of a notebook into four, and written:

AIR	WATER
FIRE	EARTH

a vast flood of information began to accrue around each of these catagories.

I began to discover parallels with my work (Eggs, Ladders, Four Elements etc.) - principally with Joyce, Pound, Yeats, and Blake, and then from other sources that they led me to. From Joyce came references to Giordano Bruno and Giambattista Vico, circular theories of time - the Four Ages of man, the Four evangelists, the Cardinal Points, and the seasons. I redrew the diagram as a circle divided into four sections. From Pound came ideas on the Zodiac, Dante, and Organic Time. That is Organic, Cyclical time as measured by Sunrise, Sunset, the Lunar months and cosmic rythms, the flow of time as we experience it: opposed to Linear Time measured off into discrete units by mechanical instruments - one way, irreversible, objective, and historical. As Pearlman points out 'Pound shows in the Cantos that only those men and societies governed by a reverence for organic time have the linear strength to resist the destructive efforts of those who live.by mechanical time.' and also.... 'Economics must be brought into harmony with the seasons, with the productive rhythms and capacities of chthonic nature and human nature both.' Which perhaps helps to explain the great success of the Chinese civilisation today in comparison with the decadence of the U.S.A. The opposite is true however for the North American Indians exterminated by the White man. The following texts were recorded recently, but are voices from a distant past.

4

....everything an Indian does is in a circle... and that is because the Power of the World always works in circles, and everything tries to be round. In the old days when we were a strong happy people, all our power came to us from the sacred hoop of the nation, and so long as the hoop was unbroken the people flourished. The flowering tree was the living centre of the hoop, and the circle of the four quarters nourished it. The East gave peace and light, the South gave warmth, the West gave rain, and the North with its cold and mighty wind gave strength and endurance. This knowledge came to us from the outer world with our religion. Everything the Power of the World does is done in a circle. The sky is round, and I have heard that the earth is round like a ball, and so are all the stars. The wind in all its greatest powers, whirls. Birds make their nests in circles, for theirs is the same religion as ours. The sun comes forth and goes down again in a circle. The moon does the same and both are round. Even the seasons form a circle in their changing, and always come back to where they were. The life of man is in a circle from childhood, and so is everything where Power moves. Our tepees were round like the nests of birds, and these were always set in a circle, the nations' hoop, where the Great Spirit meant us to hatch our children....
(Black Elk - North American Indian - shaman of the Oglala Sioux.)

MOTHER EARTH

...It is a sin to wound or cut, to tear or scratch our common mother by working at agriculture. You ask me to dig in the earth? But then when I die, she will not gather me again into her bosom. You tell me to dig up and take away the stones. Must I mutilate her flesh so as to get at her bones? Then I can never again enter into her body and be born again. You ask me to cut the grass and corn and sell them to get rich like the white man. How can I crop the hair of my mother?
(Smohalla - American Indian - shaman of the Umatillas)

In reading Yeats' 'A Vision' I found many connexions between my diagram and Yeats explanation of the gyres and the great wheel. A key phrase for me was the use to which this information should be put. When Yeats discovered his wife was writing, automatically he asked if he should give his life to explaining and piecing together the scattered sentences - the answer:'No. We have come to give you metaphors for poetry'.... which is the spirit in which this investigation and these notes were made. Not for themselves but to give a deeper background to my work. What has emerged for me after this investigation is a greater involvement with cycles of nature and a Yantra imprinted on my mind. The sort of memory system that Yeats refers to in 'A Vision'....'Some will ask whether I believe in the actual existwnce of my circuits of sun and moon. Those that include, now all recorded time in one circuit, now what Blake called "the pulsation of an artery" are plainly symbolical, but what of those that fixed, like a butterfly on a pin, to our central date, the first day of our Era, divide actual

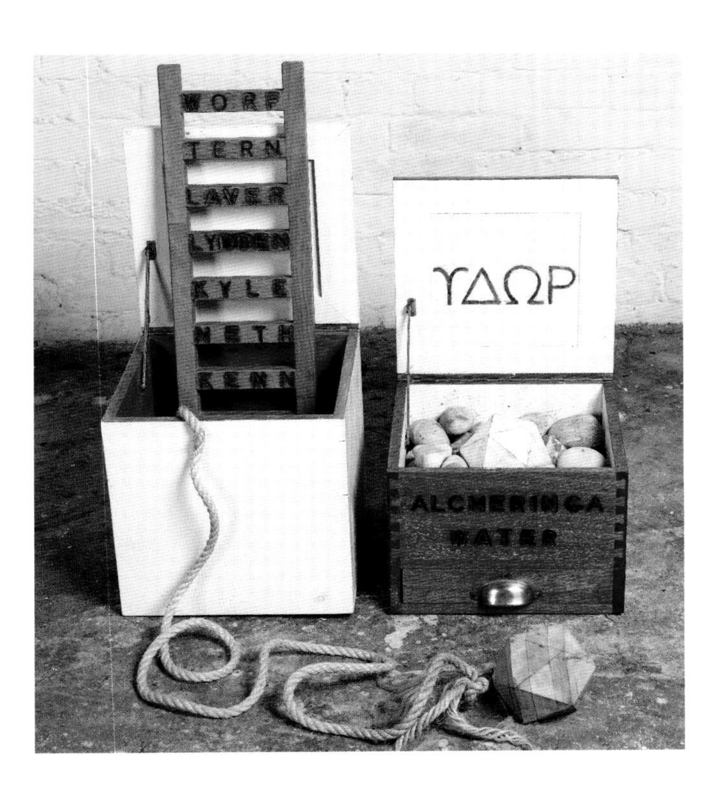

23 WATER BOX and ALCHERINGA WATER BOX, 1971–72
Wood boxes with sculptures, stones and photographs,
30.5 × 30.5 × 30.5 cm; 23 × 30.5 × 30.5 cm. Private collection

24 EARTH BOX and ALCHERINGA EARTH BOX, 1971–72
Wood boxes with sculpture, moss and photographs,
30.5 × 30.5 × 30.5 cm; 23 × 30.5 × 30.5 cm. Private collection

5

history into periods of equal length? To such a question I can but answer that if sometimes, overwhelmed by miracle as all men must be when in the midst of it, I have taken such periods literally, my reason has soon recovered; and that the system stands out clearly in my imagination I regard them as stylistic arrangements of experience comparable to the cubes in the drawing of Wyndham Lewis and to the ovoids in the sculpture of Brancusi. They have helped me to hold in a single thought reality and justice.'

This idea of complexity being held in a single thought is behind the memory systems of the Greeks revived by Giordano Bruno. The circle in the square is an image I have used for many years, but it was not until I studied the Neoplatonic and Hermetic books that I realised fully the use of the circle as a mnemonic device and a structure in art and thought, and the importance of the idea of a memory system geared to the universe. The Alchera structure is only bones, and even the arrangement of bones has emerged very slowly from images I had already been working with – and its clothing with flesh, and its life, are my actions over the last two years ending in the drawings, prints, boxes, sculptures, reliefs, and paintings.

From Blake came references to Jakob Boehme, and the Orphic writings – and I went on to collect ideas from Shamanism, Tantric Buddhism, American Indian Myths, early Chinese thought, Christian Rosenkreutz, and Alchemy, or rather the recent re-evaluation of the spiritual meaning of Alchemy by Jung and Eliade as opposed to viewing it as proto chemistry. I also found relevant thoughts in Valery and Rilke; particularly Rilke's concept of Poetry as meaning, and the concept of

the ORPHIC VOICE that speaks through the poet

Rilke says in writing of the 'Sonnets of Orpheus' that....'the fact that they suddenly, without my willing it, arose in connexion with a girl who died young, removes them still further towards the fountain of their origin; this connexion is one more relation towards the centre of that realm whose depth and influsnce we, everywhere unbounded as we are, share with the dead and those yet to come.. Nature, the things we associate with and use, are provisional and perishable; but so long as we are here they are our possession and our friendship; sharers in our trouble and gladness, just as they have been the confidants of our ancestors. Therefore, not only must all that is here not be vilified or degraded, but, just because of that very provisionality they share with us, all these apparances and things should be, in the most fervent sense, comprehended by us and transformed. Transformed? Yes, for our task is to stamp this provisional perishing earth into ourselves so deeply, so painfully and passionately, that its being may rise again, invisibly in us. We are the bees of the invisible.

6

Nous butinous eperdument le miel du visible, pour l'accumuler dans le grande ruche d'or de l'invisible.
(Rilke)

All that is visible clings to the invisible,
The audible to the inaudible
The tangible to the intangible
perhaps the thinkable to the unthinkable
(Novalis)

This view of nature.... and the view of the poet as the instrument through which the orphic voice speaks or sings – have parallels in Tibetan and Indian mysticism.

.... The forms of divine life in the universe and in nature break forth from the seer as vision, from the singer as sound, and are there in the spell of vision and sound, pure and undisguised. Their existence is the characteristic of the priestly power of the seer-poet. What sounds from his mouth is not the ordinary word, of which speech is composed. It is Mantra.
(Zimmer.)

Vedanta meditation uses Yantra, Mantra, and the cult-image (Pratina). YANTRA is a diagram for meditation – MANTRA is the verbal form – and the cult-image is the seethetic form. They are instruments of transformation... the image or work of art is meaningless except as a means to an end; that end is the attainment of an interior experience. (Yantras are often drawn on paper or sand, and then thrown away or rubbed out.

In accordance with the traditional Brahmin teaching of the Creation, he lets that which is unformed and nameless change itself into the four elements, which issue one from the other. Out of emptiness proceeds air, out of air fire, out of fire water, and finally out of water earth. Whilst he lets this process develop he brings the symbols of the four elements before his inner eye. The symbols are a white semicircle with waving banners, a red triangle with a flaming jewel, a white circle with a vessel, and a yellow square with a triangular thunderbolt at each corner. They appear from the viod and issue from each other, as the mystical syllables are their manifestations in the realm of sound. The syllable 'yam' is air and produces its equivalent symbolic image; 'ram' is fire, 'vam' is water, and 'lam' is earth. They develop out of the inner image of the syllables just as out of the syllable 'sum' rises the shining apparition of the Divine Mount Sumera, the axis of the world egg, whose jewel body has four sides, which are composed of crystal, gold, ruby, and emerald. (White, Yellow, Red, Green.) They sparkle with the colours of the four quarters of the world.
(Zimmer)

25 FIRE LADDER, AIR LADDER, WATER LADDER, EARTH LADDER, 1974. Western red cedar, 225 × 120 × 9 cm; 225 × 70 × 9 cm. Private collection

7

EARTHEARTHEARTH

The most valuable piece of information from the last few years of space travel is **the IMAGE of the EARTH**

....OUR GOLDEN FLEECE FROM COLCHIS....

....all is within us....

God has planted many secrets in man so that they lie in him like seeds in the earth. And just as the seeds burgeon from the earth in spring, so the flowers and fruits that God put in men will come to light at the appointed time.
(Paracelsus)

NO DUALITY: Intellect/Emotion as one
Mind/Body as one

all patterns in the process of patterning....

....there is no world except one that we are the picturers of....
(Olson)

ANIMA MUNDI
———
IMAGO MUNDI

GEO	Geology	
	Geography	
GE	Geomorphology	THE TERRAIN
	Geocyclic	
	Geodynamic	
GAIA	Geomancy	

The thin breathing ~~SKIN~~/~~CRUST~~/VEIL of

AIR/WATER/EARTH/FIRE that we inhabit

OUR EARTH: ORGANIC, LIVING, BREATHING, CHANGING, SACRED.

1. NOT Fuller's space-ship earth. Because it gives a totaly wrong idea that we are on a static piece of hardware and that we understand and control ourselves and it!
2. NOT even 'Ecology' because it relates too much to OIKOS (house) - but rather TEMENOLOGY (Temenos: SACRED PRECINCT) ....and also....
3. 'La nostra terra e tempio del mondo'. (Giordano Bruno - Spaccio della Bestia Trionfante. dial.3.ital.pp784-6) OUR EARTH IS THE TEMPLE OF THE WORLD.

How can the world live for us?
How can the ploughed field be changed from a patch of meaningless dirt to become the body of Mother Earth?
How can we live with nature without dominating it?

8

The pattern of volcanoes on the globe, and research under the sea, has revealed that it is not an accident that the land masses look as though they were once interlocked. We now know that the thin veil we live within, and are indivisibly linked to, is continually moving. The edges of the six major plates folding down into the athenosphere, and the athenosphere being pushed up again - one of the great CYCLES - with the CYCLE of WATER which we are part of - the exposure of rock to the action of wind and rain, the entry of water into the rocks and the freezing which cracks them, the slow buids up of humus, the cycle of water, the sweeping up of the sea water, its conversion to rain water.

CYCLE OF DAY AND NIGHT
CYCLE OF THE SEASONS
CYCLE OF THE LUNAR MONTHS

How can we enter more deeply into these cycles?

2 CLUES FROM THOMAS TRAHERNE

'The corn was Orient and Immortal Wheat, which never should be reaped, nor was sown. I thought it had stood from everlasting to everlasting. The Dust and Stones of the Street were as precious as GOLD. The Gates were at first the End of the World, The Green Trees when I saw them first through one of the Gates Transported and Ravished me; their Sweetnes and unusual Beauty made my Heart to leap, and almost mad with Extasie, they were such Strange and Wonderfull Thing.'

'You never Enjoy the World aright, till the Sea itself floweth in your veins, till you are clothed with the Heavens, and Crowned with the Stars; and Perceiv your self to be the Sole Heir of the Whole World; and more then so, because Men are in it who are evryone Sole Heirs, as well as you.'

If the objects that surround us and our actions have a sacred nature for us, the matrix of our viewing shifts to lift itself out of time without losing contact with the objects of our existence and their processes - they become transformed - they partake of the mythical without losing their physical nature - the taste of Wine, Olive, Rucola, or Basil in the mouth, trancends time; the texture of honey in the tongue, the sensation of drinking water from a mountain spring, the sound of the Yellow Oriole, or the cuckoo, the smell of Honeysuckle, your hand on the bark of an oak tree, a cat sitting upright in egyptian pose - these link us with all time.
Our imagination must be geared passionalely to the universe - to nature - (Nature including human nature as an indivisible part of the process). We must be always aware that we are part of the cycles of continual change in a thin breathing moving veil of air, water and earth, our temple sphere.

I think of Art as a tool of understanding, an instrument of transormation to put yourself in harmony with the world and life.

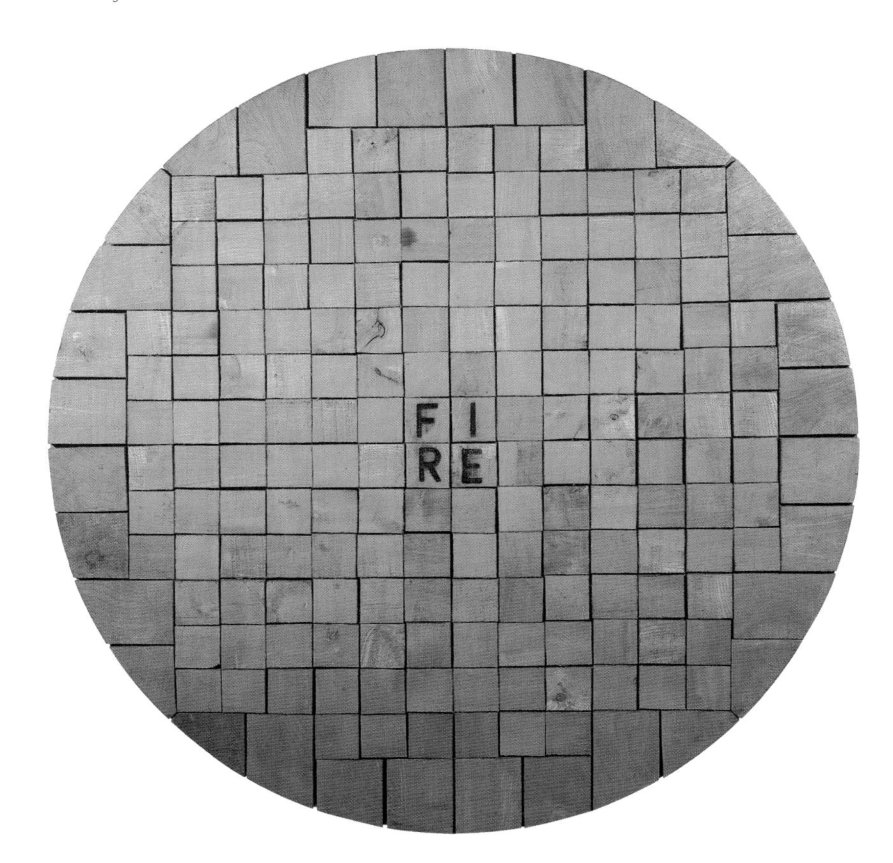

26 FIREWHEEL, 1974. Elm, 183 × 183 cm. Private collection

27 TREE ALPHABET, 1973. Oil on wood, 248 × 142 cm. Private collection

28 ΛΑΒΥΡΙΝΘΟΣ JULIAN'S BOWER, 1974. Elm, 249 × 219 cm. Private collection

29 ΛΑΒΥΡΙΝΘΟΣ TROJAN DOOR, 1974. Elm, 239 × 178 cm. Private collection

30 EARTHCUBE, 1979. Earth pigments on wood relief, 208 × 208 cm. Private collection

31 THE FLAYING OF MARSYAS C, 1989. Oil on canvas on wood relief, 221 × 198 cm. Private collection

32 LIKNON 3, 1987. Oil on canvas on wood relief, 197 × 197 cm. Tate. Presented by the Trustees of the Chantrey Bequest, 1988

33 MOON SIGNATURES, 1985. Oil and silver leaf on canvas, 254 × 194 cm. Waddington Galleries Ltd

34 SUN SIGNATURES, 1985. Oil and gold leaf on canvas, 254 × 194 cm. Waddington Galleries Ltd

LE CRETE SENESI

These works take their name from the hills around Siena that can be seen from the old main road, the Via Lauretana, south to Asciano; from the white road to San Vito and Monte a Castello; and from the other road south towards San Quirico, Radicofani and the Abbey of Monte Oliveto Maggiore. These hills can be seen in the paintings of Sassetta, Giovanni di Paolo, Simone Martini and Lorenzetti in the Palazzo Pubblico in Siena. The tops of these hills, washed away by rain, reveal small, chalky white cones called 'biancane'; steeper cliffs are called 'balze'. The rolling hillsides are divided by water courses, 'borri', which become torrents, carving out small valleys or 'calanchi'. These torrents later become the larger rivers that divide the region – the Merse, Arbia, Orcia and Ombrone – along which lie the early Etruscan settlements near Asciano, Murlo and Serre di Rapolano, from whose clay, interspersed with huge wedges of Travertine marble, rise hot springs. The names of the works are taken from these rivers and from place names that echo history and the landscape: Sasso, Colle, Monte – stone, hill, mountain. The works parallel the action of time and weather that created the worn, moulded, carved and eroded character of the landscape, sculpted over centuries by rain, wind, vegetation and cultivation. From the rock, split by frost and ice, comes the fertility of the topsoil whose insect and plant life, trees and crops give this part of Tuscany its forms and colours: the dark green of rows of cypresses against the silver-green of olive trees; and soil turned by the plough to reveal the colours of the earth pigments of the region that have been used for centuries by painters, and are still used today: the ferric oxides which give yellow, gold, brown and red ochres, and raw and burnt sienna.

Joe Tilson

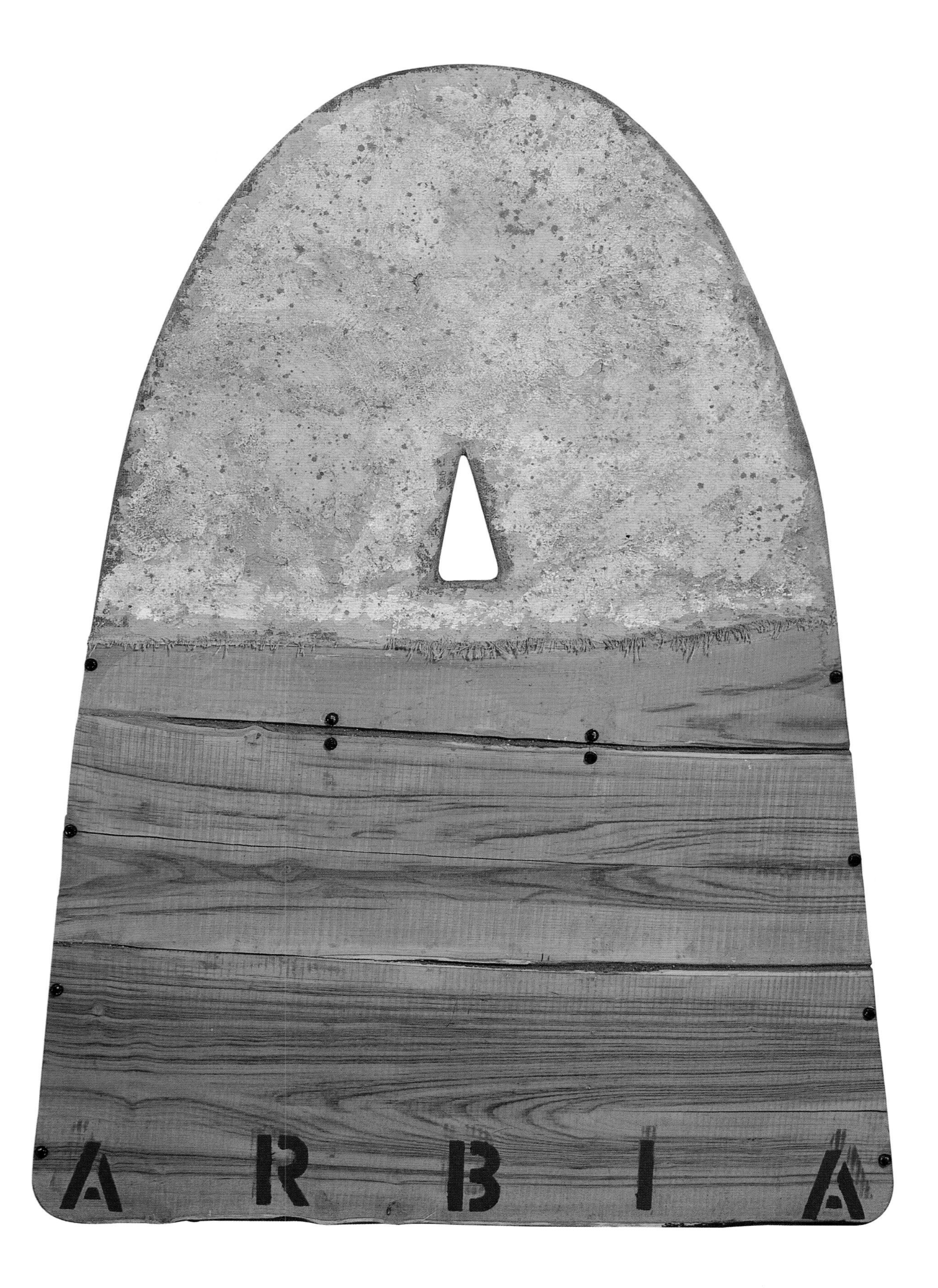

35 LE CRETE SENESI, ARBIA, 1993. Oil on canvas on wood relief, 166 × 120 cm. Private collection

36 LE CRETE SENESI, SAN QUIRICO, 1993. Oil on canvas on wood relief, 226 × 179 cm. Private collection

37 LE CRETE SENESI, SANT'ANTIMO, 1993. Oil on canvas on wood relief, 216 × 180 cm. Private collection

38 LE CRETE SENESI, SAN VITO, 1993. Oil on canvas on wood relief, 218 × 178 cm. Private collection

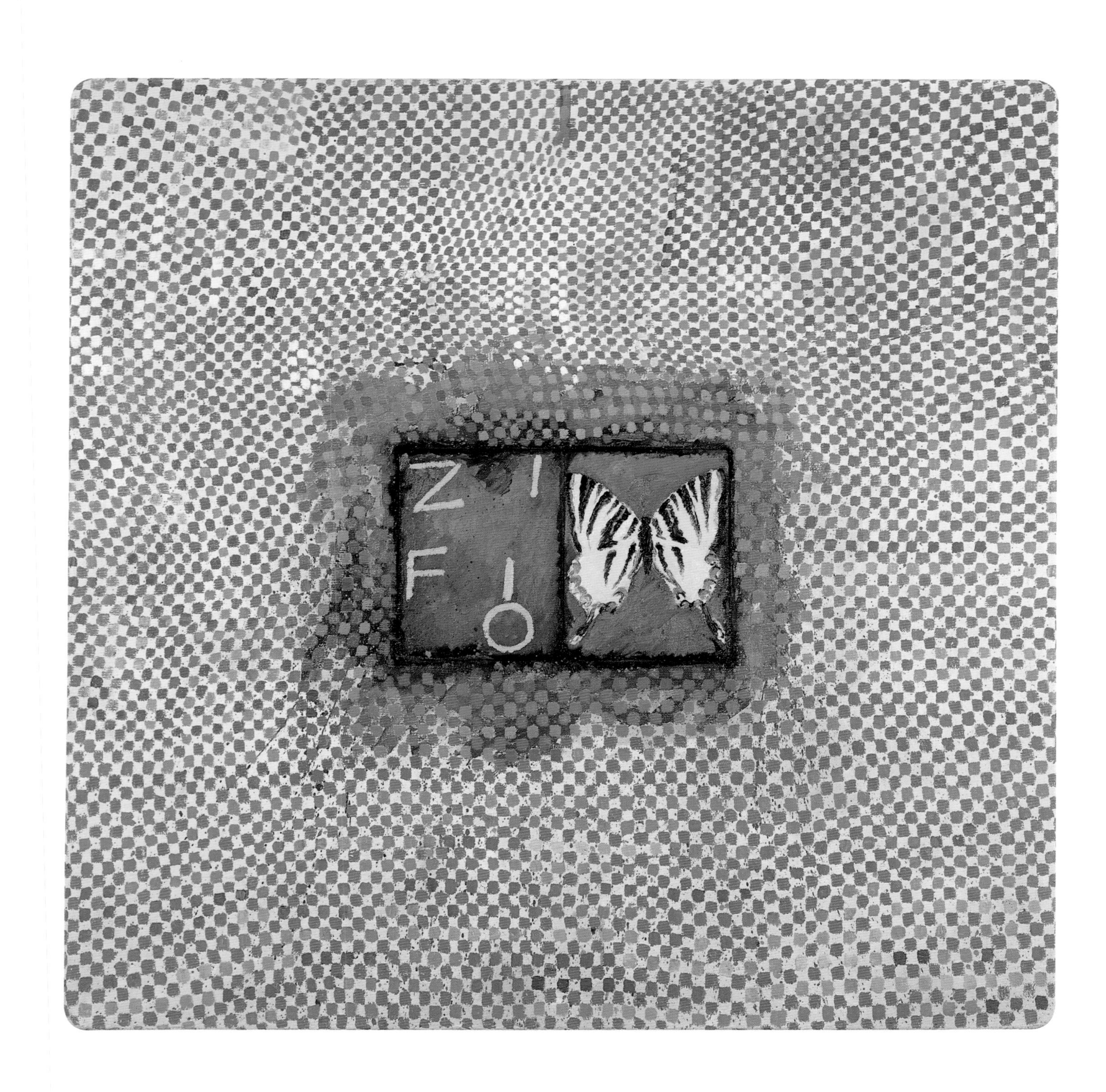

39 CONJUNCTION SWALLOWTAIL, ZIFIO, 1997. Oil on canvas on wood relief, 183 × 184 cm. Private collection

40 CONJUNCTION LAMON, 1997. Oil on canvas on wood relief, 154 × 153 cm. Private collection

41 CONJUNCTION THE NETS, 1997
Oil on canvas on wood relief,
153 × 153 cm. Private collection

42 CONJUNCTION GOLDEN ORIOLE, ZETA,
1998. Oil on canvas on wood relief,
122 × 152 cm. Private collection

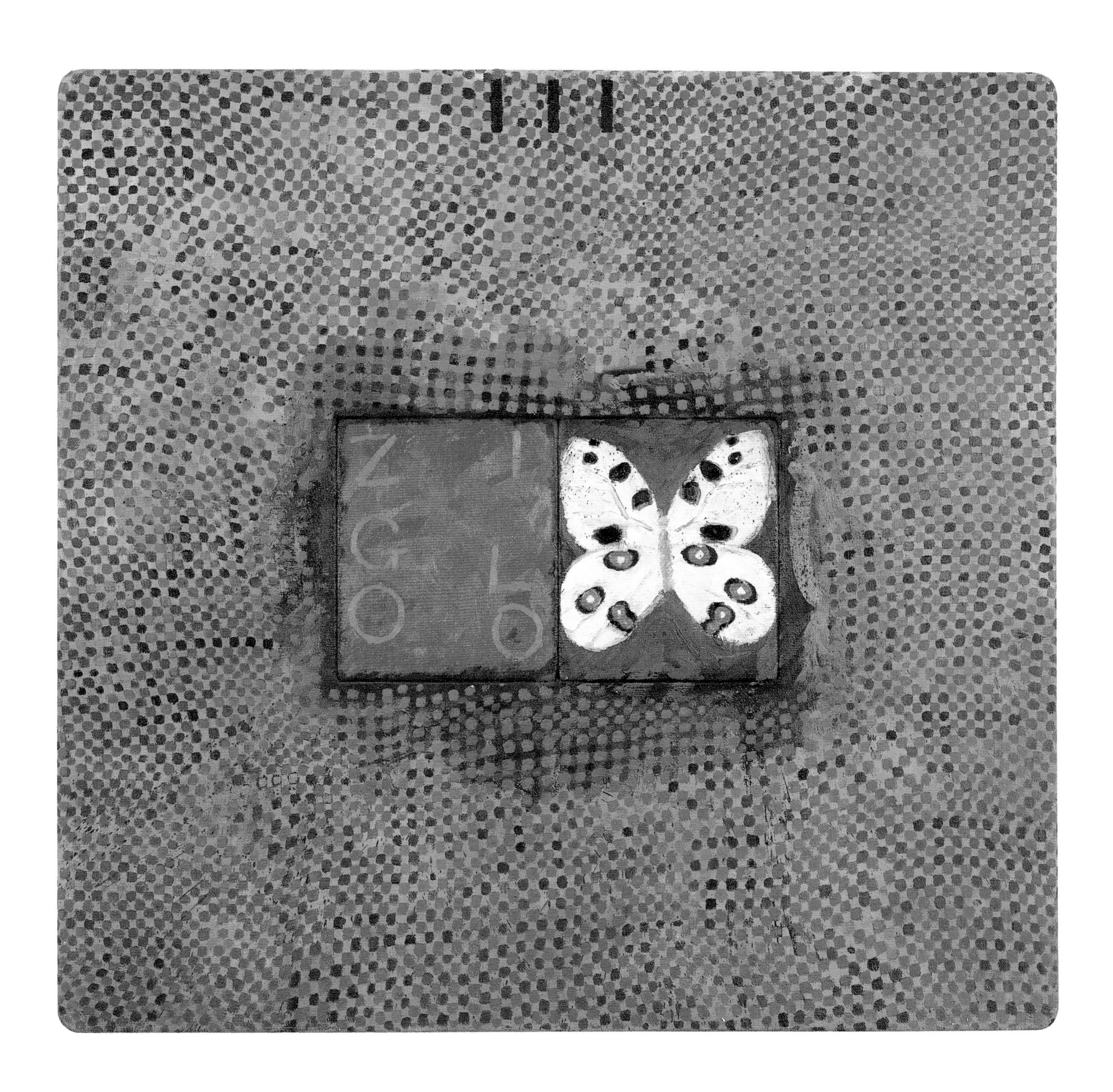

43 CONJUNCTION APOLLO, ZIGOLO, 1997. Oil on canvas on wood relief, 183 × 184 cm. Private collection

BIOGRAPHY

Joe Tilson was born in London in 1928. Having worked as a carpenter and joiner from 1944 to 1946, he served in the RAF until 1949. Following his National Service, he went to St Martin's School of Art (with Leon Kossoff and Frank Auerbach) and in 1952 to the Royal College of Art (with Peter Blake and Richard Smith). In 1955, after winning the Rome Prize, he lived and worked in Rome where he met Joslyn Morton, who was studying with Marino Marini at the Brera in Milan. They lived together at Cefalù in Sicily and, in 1956, were married in Venice from their studio in Casa Frollo on the Giudecca. After some months in Catalonia with Peter Blake, they returned to London where Tilson taught at St Martin's School of Art from 1958 to 1963, then at the Slade School of Art, University College, London; at King's College, Newcastle-upon-Tyne; at the School of Visual Arts, New York; and the Hochschule für Bildende Künste, Hamburg.

For more than forty years Tilson has been making and exhibiting paintings, constructions, reliefs, prints and multiples. Originally associated with the British Pop Art movement in the early 1960s, he was soon led in a different direction by his deeply held convictions and his dissatisfaction with the technology and industrial 'progress' of the consumer society. 'Art', Tilson has written, 'is a symbolic discourse of which mankind alone is capable...I think of art as a tool of understanding, an instrument of transformation to put yourself in harmony with the world and with life... The basic given data of experience and the physiological and pyschological aspects of procreation, birth, growth and death remain relatively unchanged.' As André Gide wrote, 'Toutes choses sont dites déjà; mais comme personne n'écoute, il faut toujours recommencer.' The themes Tilson chooses for his work aspire to transcend time and cut across cultures, to communicate the sacred in nature via references to pre-classical mythology, the North American Indians, the Dream Time of the Australian Aboriginals, and alchemy. Modular structuring devices – the letters of the alphabet, the days of the week, the circular mnemonic devices of *Alchera* which relate to the four Cardinal points, to the four Elements and to the four Seasons, the lunar months, labyrinths, ladders, words, symbols – are assembled in matrices layered with complex universal meaning.

A contemporary of Frank Auerbach, Leon Kossoff, R. B. Kitaj, Peter Blake, Allen Jones, Patrick Caulfield and David Hockney (all students of the Royal College of Art), Tilson first had his works exhibited internationally in 1964 at the XXXII Venice Biennale. A retrospective exhibition at the Museum Boijmans van Beuningen in Rotterdam was also shown in Belgium and Italy in 1971. Other retrospectives took place at the Vancouver Art Gallery in 1979, and at the Arnolfini Gallery, Bristol, in 1984. He has also exhibited in numerous public and private collections.

Tilson's first one-man exhibition took place at the Marlborough Gallery, London, in 1962. He continued to exhibit at their galleries in New York and Rome until 1977 when he joined the Waddington Galleries. He is at present represented by the Beaux Arts Gallery and the Alan Cristea Gallery in London, and by the Giò Marconi Gallery in Milan. In 1985, Joe Tilson was elected to membership of the Royal Academy of Arts, London.

Tilson has three children, Jake, Anna and Sophy, and lives with his wife Jos in London. During the last thirty-three years he has spent several months of each year at their house in the hills near Cortona in Tuscany.

Recent exhibitions include reliefs and sculptures in maiolica and terracotta made over the last ten years with the Cooperativa Ceramica d'Imola at the Bologna Art Fair, and *Le Crete Senesi* at the Giò Marconi Gallery, Milan, the Pinacoteca Macerata, and then the Palazzo Pubblico, Siena, for which city he was invited to paint the prize banner for the Palio of 1996. That year he won the 'Grand Prix d'Honneur' at the Biennale of Ljubljana, followed in 1997 by a retrospective exhibition of prints at the Cankarjev Dom, Ljubljana.

Tilson's one-man exhibition 'Selected Works' was shown at the Castello Doria, Porto Venere, in 1999. In the same year 'I Tilson', an exhibition of terracottas by his wife Jos and his own *Conjunctions*, was held at the Palazzo Pubblico, Siena. The exhibition 'Conjunctions' subsequently travelled to the Galleria Comunale d'Arte, Cesena, and the Pinacoteca Civica, Follonica, in 2000. In 2001, selected retrospective exhibitions were organised at Castelbasso and at the Giò Marconi Gallery, Milan, and he was elected Associate of the Accademia di San Luca in Rome. In 2002, as well as his exhibition in the Sackler Wing at the Royal Academy of Arts, an exhibition of his prints will take place at the Alan Cristea Gallery and recent paintings will be shown at the Beaux Arts Gallery.

SELECT BIBLIOGRAPHY

Pages, exh. cat., Marlborough Fine Art, London, March – April 1970

Joe Tilson, *Alchera*, Pollenza-Macerata, 1976

Arturo Carlo Quintavalle, *Tilson* (preface by Pierre Restany), Milan, 1977

Gillo Dorfles, *Maestri contemporanei: Tilson*, Milan, 1982

Antonio del Guercio, *A Light from Eleusis*, Milan, 1991

Maurizio Fagiolo dell'Arco, *Opere recenti: Extra Mœnia*, Todi, 1992

Michael Compton and Marco Livingstone, *Tilson*, London and New York, 1992

Enrico Crispolti, *Terracotta e maiolica: sculture e rilievi*, Imola, 1995

Omar Calabrese, Mauro Civai, Enrico Crispolti, Ilaria Vanni and Giandomenico Semeraro, *Le Crete Senesi*, exh. cat., Palazzo Pubblico, Siena, 1995

Mauro Civai, Alessandro Falassi and Marco Pierini, *I Tilson: Conjunctions*, exh. cat., Palazzo Pubblico, Siena, 1999

Silvia Pegoraro, *Alchimie dei simboli*, exh. cat., Castelbasso, 2001

Mel Gooding, *Tilson*, exh. cat., Beaux Arts Gallery, London, 2002

LIST OF WORKS

1 WOOD RELIEF NO. 17, 1961. Wood, 125 × 95 × 8 cm. Tate. Purchased 1962

2 FOR JAKE AND ANNA, 1961. Oil on wood relief, 96.5 × 127 cm. Private collection

3 A–Z BOX OF FRIENDS AND FAMILY, 1963. Mixed media, 233 × 152 cm. Private collection

4 GEOMETRY? 3, 1964. Oil and acrylic on wood relief, 188 × 188 cm. Private collection

5 ASTRONAUT PUZZLE, 1963. Oil on wood relief, 132 × 102 × 8 cm. Collection Emilio Carpeggiani, Verona

6 KEY BOX, 1963. Oil on wood relief, 182 × 144 × 27 cm. Private collection, Milan

7 NINE ELEMENTS, 1963. Kandy, pearl and acrylic on wood relief, 259 × 183 cm. Scottish National Gallery of Modern Art, Edinburgh. Purchased 1983

8 21ST, 1963. Oil on canvas and board, 170 × 121 × 3 cm. Renata Pellerano, Modena

9 TRANSPARENCY, THE FIVE SENSES: TASTE, 1969. Screenprinted and vacuum-formed acrylic sheet, 147.5 × 147.5 cm. Tate. Presented by Marlborough Graphics through the Institute of Contemporary Prints, 1970

10 LOOK!, 1964. Oil, acrylic on wood relief, 186.69 × 195.58 × 7.62 cm. Collection Walker Art Center, Minneapolis Art Center Acquisition Fund, 1966

11 VOX BOX, 1963. Oil on wood relief, 153 × 122 cm. Tate. Purchased 1976

12 SKY, GREEK CROSS AND DODECAGON, 1967. Tri-chromatic screen and polyurethane on wood relief, 122 × 244 × 10 cm. Private collection

13 ZIKKURAT 7, 1967. Oil and acrylic on wood relief, 187 × 295 × 14 cm. Arts Council Collection, Hayward Gallery, London

14 ZIKKURAT 3, 1967. Oil and acrylic on wood relief, 216 × 216 cm. Private collection

15 ZIKKURAT 9, 1967. Oil and acrylic on wood relief, 214 × 214 × 14 cm. Private collection

16 PAGE 16, ECOLOGY, FIRE, AIR, WATER, EARTH, 1969. Screen and oil on canvas on wood relief, 169 × 169 cm. Private collection

17 PAGE 8, BLACK DWARF, 1969. Screen on canvas on wood relief, 187 × 126 cm. Private collection

18 PAGE 19, HE, SHE & IT, 1969–70. Screen and oil on canvas on wood relief, 187 × 126 cm. Private collection

19 PAGE 18, MUHAMMAD SPEAKS, 1969–70. Screen and oil on canvas on wood relief, 187 × 126 cm. Private collection

20 MNEMONIC DEVICE, 1973. Oil on wood panel, 211 × 211 cm. Private collection

21 FIRE BOX and ALCHERINGA FIRE BOX, 1971–72. Wood boxes with wood sculpture, straw and photographs, 30.5 × 30.5 × 30.5 cm; 23 × 30.5 × 30.5 cm. Private collection

22 AIR BOX and ALCHERINGA AIR BOX, 1971–72. Wood boxes with sculpture, feathers and photographs, 30.5 × 30.5 × 30.5 cm; 23 × 30.5 × 30.5 cm. Private collection

23 WATER BOX and ALCHERINGA WATER BOX, 1971–72. Wood boxes with sculptures, stones and photographs, 30.5 × 30.5 × 30.5 cm; 23 × 30.5 × 30.5 cm. Private collection

24 EARTH BOX and ALCHERINGA EARTH BOX, 1971–72. Wood boxes with sculpture, moss and photographs, 30.5 × 30.5 × 30.5 cm; 23 × 30.5 × 30.5 cm. Private collection

25 FIRE LADDER, AIR LADDER, WATER LADDER, EARTH LADDER, 1974. Western red cedar, 225 × 120 × 7 cm; 225 × 70 × 9 cm. Private collection

26 FIREWHEEL, 1974. Elm, 183 × 183 cm. Private collection

27 TREE ALPHABET, 1973. Oil on wood, 248 × 142 cm. Private collection

28 ΛΑΒΥΡΙΝΘΟΣ JULIAN'S BOWER, 1974. Elm, 249 × 219 cm. Private collection

29 ΛΑΒΥΡΙΝΘΟΣ TROJAN DOOR, 1974. Elm, 239 × 178 cm. Private collection

30 EARTHCUBE, 1979. Earth pigments on wood relief, 208 × 208 cm. Private collection

31 THE FLAYING OF MARSYAS C, 1989. Oil on canvas on wood relief, 221 × 198 cm. Private collection

32 LIKNON 3, 1987. Oil on canvas on wood relief, 197 × 197 cm. Tate. Presented by the Trustees of the Chantrey Bequest, 1988

33 MOON SIGNATURES, 1985. Oil and silver leaf on canvas, 254 × 194 cm. Waddington Galleries Ltd

34 SUN SIGNATURES, 1985. Oil and gold leaf on canvas, 254 × 194 cm. Waddington Galleries Ltd

35 LE CRETE SENESI, ARBIA, 1993. Oil on canvas on wood relief, 166 × 120 cm. Private collection

36 LE CRETE SENESI, SAN QUIRICO, 1993. Oil on canvas on wood relief, 226 × 179 cm. Private collection

37 LE CRETE SENESI, SANT'ANTIMO, 1993. Oil on canvas on wood relief, 216 × 180 cm. Private collection

38 LE CRETE SENESI, SAN VITO, 1993. Oil on canvas on wood relief, 218 × 178 cm. Private collection

39 CONJUNCTION SWALLOWTAIL, ZIFIO, 1997. Oil on canvas on wood relief, 183 × 184 cm. Private collection

40 CONJUNCTION LAMON, 1997. Oil on canvas on wood relief, 154 × 153 cm. Private collection

41 CONJUNCTION THE NETS, 1997. Oil on canvas on wood relief, 153 × 153 cm. Private collection

42 CONJUNCTION GOLDEN ORIOLE, ZETA, 1998. Oil on canvas on wood relief, 122 × 152 cm. Private collection

43 CONJUNCTION APOLLO, ZIGOLO, 1997. Oil on canvas on wood relief, 183 × 184 cm. Private collection

ROYAL ACADEMY TRUST

Major Benefactors
The Trustees of the Royal Academy Trust would like to thank all those who have been exceedingly generous over a number of years in support of the galleries, the exhibitions, the conservation of the Collections, the Library, the Royal Academy Schools and the education programme:

HM The Queen
The 29th May 1961 Charitable Trust
The Annenberg Foundation
The Annie Laurie Aitken Charitable Trust
American Associates of the Royal Academy Trust
The Annenberg Foundation
Barclays Bank
Mr and Mrs Sid R Bass
B.A.T. Industries plc
Tom Bendhem
Brenda M Benwell-Lejeune
John Frye Bourne
British Telecom
The Brown Foundation Inc
Mr Raymond M Burton CBE
Sir Trevor Chinn CVO and Lady Chinn
The Trustees of the Clore Foundation
The John S Cohen Foundation
Mr Edwin L Cox
Sir Harry and Lady Djanogly
The Dulverton Trust
Alfred Dunhill Limited
The John Ellerman Foundation
The Eranda Foundation
Ernst and Young
Esso UK plc
Esmée Fairbairn Charitable Trust
Mr and Mrs Eugene V Fife
Walter Fitch III
Mrs Henry Ford II
The Honorable Amalia Lacroze de Fortabat
The Foundation for Sport and the Arts
Friends of the Royal Academy
The Getty Grant Program
Glaxo Holdings plc
Diane and Guilford Glazer
Jack and Grete Goldhill
Maurice and Laurence Goldman
The late Dr Armand Hammer
Mr and Mrs Jocelin Harris
The Philip and Pauline Harris Charitable Trust
The Hayward Foundation
The Hearst Corporation
The Drue Heinz Trust
The Horace W Goldsmith Foundation
Heritage Lottery Fund
IBM United Kingdom Limited
The Idlewild Trust
The JP Jacobs Charitable Trust
Lord and Lady Jacobs
The Japan Foundation
Gabrielle Jungels-Winkler Foundation
Mr and Mrs Donald P Kahn
The Kresge Foundation
The Kresse Foundation
The Lankelly Foundation
Mr John S Latsis
Mrs Katherine K Lawrence
The Leverhulme Trust
Lex Service plc
The Linbury Trust
Sir Sydney Lipworth QC and Lady Lipworth
The Henry Luce Foundation
John Madejski
Her Majesty's Government
The Manifold Trust
Mr and Mrs John L Marion
Marks and Spencer
Mr and Mrs Jack C Massey
Mr Hamish Maxwell
Ronald and Rita McAulay
Mrs John P McGrath
McKinsey and Company Inc
The Estate of Paul Mellon KBE
The Mercers' Company
The Monument Trust
The Henry Moore Foundation
The Moorgate Trust Fund
Robin Moss
Museums and Galleries Improvement Fund
National Westminster Bank
Mrs Nancy B Negley
New Opportunities Fund
Stavros S Niarchos
Ms Diane A Nixon
The Otemae College
The Peacock Trust
The Pennycress Trust
PF Charitable Trust
The Pilgrim Trust
Leon B Polsky and Cynthia Hazen Polsky
The Edith and Ferdinand Porjes Trust
Rio Tinto plc
John A Roberts FRIBA
The Ronson Foundation
The Rose Foundation
Rothmans International plc
Mrs Arthur M Sackler
Mrs Jean Sainsbury
The Saison Foundation
The Basil Samuel Charitable Trust
Mrs Louisa S Sarofim
Sea Containers Ltd
Shell UK Limited
Miss Dasha Shenkman
William and Maureen Shenkman
The Archie Sherman Charitable Trust
Ms Kathleen D Smith
The Martin and Toni Sosnoff Foundation
The Starr Foundation
Mr and Mrs Robert Lee Sterling Jr
Sir Hugh Sykes DL
Alfred Taubman
Mr and Mrs Vernon Taylor Jr
Sir Anthony and Lady Tennant
The Eugene and Clare Thaw Charitable Trust
Ware and Edythe Travelstead
The Trusthouse Charitable Foundation
The Douglas Turner Trust
Unilever plc
The Weldon UK Charitable Trust
The Welton Foundation
Garry H Weston and the Weston family
The Honorable John C Whitehead
Mr and Mrs Frederick B Whittemore
The Malcolm Hewitt Wiener Foundation
The Maurice Wohl Charitable Foundation
The Wolfson Foundation
and others who wish to remain anonymous

Benefactors
The Trustees of the Royal Academy Trust would like to thank all those who have recently supported the galleries, the exhibitions, the conservation of the Collections, the Library, the Royal Academy Schools or the education programme:

Benjamin West Group Donors
Patron
The Hon Raymond G H Seitz

Chairman
The Hon Barbara S Thomas

Donors
Lady Adamson
Sir Rudolph and Lady Agnew
Michael and Barbara Anderson
Mrs Alan Artus
Mrs Davis Bader
Mr and Mrs Thomas J Berger
Mr and Mrs Mark Booth
Mrs Adrian Bowden
Mr and Mrs Robert Bowman
Mr and Mrs Charles Brocklebank
A Chilcott Fawcett
Mr and Mrs Paul Collins
Mrs Joan Curci
Mr and Mrs C R Dammers
Mrs Sheryl Daniels-Young
Mr and Mrs Domenico De Sole
Mr and Mrs David Diwik
Mr and Mrs Robert L Forbes
The David Gill Memorial Fund
Mr and Mrs John Gore
Mr and Mrs Abel Halpern
Mrs M R Hambro
Mr Andrew Hawkins
Mrs Susan Hayden
Robin Heller Moss
Mr Paul Josefowitz
Sir Paul Judge
Mr and Mrs Richard Kaufman
Rona and Robert Kiley
Tom Larsen, Holt Value Associates
Mr Charles G Lubar
Ms Claudine B Malone
Mr and Mrs Bruce McLaren
Mr and Mrs Philip Mengel
Mr and Mrs Edward Miller
Mr and Mrs Donald Moore
Mr Neil Osborn and Ms Holly Smith
Sir William and Lady Purves
Mr and Mrs Nicolas Rohatyn
Mrs Sylvia B Scheuer
Mr and Mrs Stuart L Scott
Mr and Mrs Paul Shang
Mrs Tara Stack
Susan and Don Starr
John and Sheila Stoller
Barbara and Allen Thomas
Mrs Kathryn Uhde
Michael and Yvonne Uva
Mr and Mrs Jeffrey Weingarten
Mr Randall J Willette
Mr and Mrs John D Winter
and others who wish to remain anonymous

Collection Patrons Group
Miss B A Battersby
Mrs Helena Frost
David and Maggi Gordon
Idlewild Trust
The Leche Trust
The Lesley David Trust
Mr Lowell J Libson
Pamela Littman JP
Robin Heller Moss
Mrs Graham Reddish
Joseph Strong Frazer Trust
and others who wish to remain anonymous

Education Patrons Group
Mr Tom Bendhem
David and Janice Blackburn
The Goldsmiths' Company Charities
The Kobler Trust
John Lyon's Charity
The Mercers' Company
The Merrell Foundation
The Millichope Foundation
JP Morgan Fleming Foundation
Mr and Mrs J A Pye's Charitable Settlement
Mrs Jean Sainsbury
Miss Joanna Trollope OBE
The Walcot Educational Foundation
The Woo Charitable Foundation
and others who wish to remain anonymous

Exhibitions Patrons Group
President
Mr Garry Weston

Co-Chairmen
Mrs John Burns
Sir Trevor Chinn CVO
The Hon Mrs Anne Collins

Gold Patrons
The 29th May 1961 Charitable Trust
Mrs David Allen
Lord and Lady Attenborough
Ivor Braka
Dr Christopher Brown
Mr and Mrs John Burns
Mr Raymond M Burton CBE
C H K Charities Limited
Sir Trevor and Lady Chinn
The Hon Mrs Anne Collins
Mr and Mrs David Diwik
Mr A C Gallagher
The Robert Gavron Charitable Trust
Jacqueline and Michael Gee
David and Maggi Gordon
The Gosling Foundation
Mrs Sue Hammerson
Mrs Gabrielle Jungels-Winkler
Mr and Mrs Donald P Kahn
Mr and Mrs Joseph Karaviotis
The Kreitman Foundation
The Kirby Laing Foundation
EFG Private Bank Limited
The Lady Lever of Manchester
Sir Sydney Lipworth QC and Lady Lipworth
Mr and Mrs Ronald Lubner
The P F Charitable Trust
The Rayne Foundation
Mr John A Roberts FRIBA
Mrs Eliana de Faria
Mr and Mrs Edward Miller
Paul and Alison Myners
Mr and Mrs Nicolas Rohatyn
Mrs Coral Samuel CBE
Ms Pierrette Schlettwein
Mrs Stella Shawzin
Mr and Mrs Richard Simmons
Mrs Roama Spears
Sir Anthony and Lady Tennant
Eugene V and Clare E Thaw Charitable Trust
Roger and Jennifer Wingate
Mr and Mrs Ronald W Zeghibe
Mr and Mrs Michael Zilkha

Silver Patrons
Mr and Mrs Paul Baines
The Peter Boizot Foundation
Alain and Marie Boublil
Mrs Adrian Bowden
Mrs Elie R Brihi
Lady Brown
Sir James and Lady Butler
Mr and Mrs P H G Cadbury
A Chilcott Fawcett
Mr and Mrs G L Collins
Mr and Mrs Paul Collins
Stephen and Marion Cox
Mr and Mrs Patrick Doherty
Mr and Mrs Maurice Dwek
Mr and Mrs Gerald Fogel
Mrs Helena Frost
Mr and Mrs James Gourlay of Kincraig
Charles and Kaaren Hale
Mr and Mrs Abel Halpern
Mr and Mrs Jocelin Harris
Mrs Susan Hayden
The Headley Trust
Mr and Mrs Alan Hobart
Mr and Mrs Jon Hunt
Mr Jonathon E Lyons
Fiona Mactaggart
Michael Nyman
Sir William and Lady Purves
Mrs Jean Redman-Brown
Mr and Mrs Gerry Robinson
Sophie and David Shalit
Mr and Mrs Clive Sherling
James and Alyson Spooner
Mrs Tara Stack
Mr and the Hon Mrs Richard Szpiro
Barbara and Allen Thomas
Miss Joanna Trollope OBE
Mr and Mrs Anthony Weldon
Mrs Linda M Williams

Bronze Patrons
Mr and Mrs Gerald Acher
Lady Adamson
Mrs Denise Adeane
Mrs Annabel Agace
Sir Rudolph and Lady Agnew
Mr and Mrs V Alaghband
Dr M Al-Ali
Ms Huda Al-Rasheed
Mr and the Hon Mrs Michael Alen-Buckley
Mr Peter Allinson
Mrs Elizabeth Alston
The Earl and Countess of Ancram
Michael and Barbara Anderson
Mr Zeev Aram
Mrs Alan Artus
Mrs Davis Bader
Mr Stephen Bampfylde
Jane Barker
Mr Stephen Barry
James M Bartos
The Duke of Beaufort
Mrs Wendy Becker Payton
Dr Sheilah D Bell
Tom Bendhem
Mr and Mrs Thomas J Berger
Mrs William Berger
Mrs Vanessa Bernstein
Mrs Frederick Bienstock
Mr Mark Birley
Sir Victor and Lady Blank
Mr and Mrs George Bloch
Mr and Mrs K E Boas
Mr and Mrs Mark Booth
Mr and Mrs Robert Bowman
Mr Peter Bowring CBE
Mr and Mrs Michael Bradley
Mr and Mrs William Brake
The Britto Foundation
Mr and Mrs Charles Brocklebank
Mr and Mrs Charles Brown
Jeremy Brown
Mrs Ian Buckley-Sharp
Marlene Burston
Mrs Richard Burton
Mr and Mrs P H G Cadbury
Mrs Lily Cantor
Mr F A A Carnwath CBE
Jean and Eric Cass
The Marquise de Cérenville
Mr Tim Chenevix-Trench
Ms Carol Chetta
John Chiene
Mr and Mrs T E Childs
Mrs Nicola Clark
Mrs Denise Cohen
Mr Ed Cohen
Carlo Colombotti
Neville and Carole Conrad Charitable Trust
David J and Jennifer A Cooke
Corona Extra Beer
Tom Corrigan
John C L Cox CBE
Mrs Joan Curci
Mr and Mrs C R Dammers
Ms Sheryl Daniels-Young
Mr and Mrs Hans de Gier
Peter and Kate De Haan
The de Laszlo Foundation
Anne Dell Provost
Mr and Mrs Domenico De Sole
Sir Philip Dowson PPRA and Lady Dowson
John Drummond FCSD HON DES RCA
Mr and Mrs Peter Ellis
Giuseppe Eskenazi
Mr and Mrs John and Fausta Eskenazi
The European Foundation
Mr and Mrs Nicholas Earles
John and Tawna Farmer
Mary Fedden RA
Mrs Juliet Fenton
Mr and Mrs Bryan Ferry
Mrs Donatella Flick
Flying Colours Gallery
Mr and Mrs George Fokschaner
Mr and Mrs Robert L Forbes
Mrs Edwin Fox
Cyril Freedman
Mr Monty Freedman

Michael and Clara Freeman
A Fulton Company Limited
Jacqueline and Jonathan Gestetner
The David Gill Memorial Fund
Sir Nicholas and Lady Goodison's
Charitable Settlement
Mr and Mrs John Gore
Lady Gosling
Nicholas Gould and Rachel Selzer
Mrs Michael Green
Mr and Mrs Thomas Griffin
Mr and Mrs Clifford J Gundle
Mrs M R Hambro
David and Lella Harris
The Harris Family
Mr Andrew Hawkins
David and Lesley Haynes
Michael and Morven Heller
Robin Heller Moss
Mrs Margarita Hernandez
Mr and Mrs J Hodkinson
Anne Holmes-Drewry
Dr and Mrs Allan J Horan
Mr and Mrs Ken Howard
Mrs Sue Howes and Mr Greg Dyke
Mr and Mrs Allan Hughes
Mrs Pauline Hyde
Simone Hyman
Mr Oliver Iny
Sir Martin and Lady Jacomb
Mr and Mrs Ian Jay
Harold and Valerie Joels
Mr and Mrs David Josefowitz
Mr Paul Josefowitz
Sir Paul Judge
Mr and Mrs Richard Kaufman
Mr and Mrs Laurence Kelly
Rona and Robert Kiley
Mr D H Killick
Mr and Mrs James Kirkman
Mr and Mrs F Lance Isham
Tom Larsen, Holt Value Associates
Mr George Lengvari
Colette and Peter Levy
Sir Christopher and Lady Lewinton
Susan Linaker
Mrs Livingstone
Miss R Lomax-Simpson
Mr and Mrs Mark Loveday
Mr Charles G Lubar
Richard and Rose Luce
Mrs Gertie Lurie
Mr and Mrs Eskandar Maleki
Ms Claudine B Malone
Dr Abraham Marcus
Mr and Mrs M Margulies
Marsh Christian Trust
R C Martin
Mr and Mrs Stephen Mather
Pamela and Jack Maxwell
Mrs M C W McCann
Mr and Mrs Andrew McKinna
Mr and Mrs Bruce McLaren
Mr and Mrs Philip Mengel
The Mercers' Company
Lt Col L S Michael OBE
Mr and Mrs Donald Moore
Mr and Mrs Peter Morgan
Mr and Mrs I Morrison
The Mulberry Trust
Mr and Mrs Carl Anton Muller
Mr and Mrs Elis Nemes
John Nickson and Simon Rew
N Peal Cashmere
Mr Bruce Oldfield OBE
Mr and Mrs Simon Oliver
Mr Neil Osborn and Ms Holly Smith
Sir Peter Osborne and Lady Osborne
Mr Michael Palin
Mr and Mrs Vincenzo Palladino
Mr and Mrs Gerald Parkes
John Pattisson
Mr and Mrs D J Peacock
The Pennycress Trust
Miss Karen Phillipps
Mr Godfrey Pilkington
George and Carolyn Pincus
Mr and Mrs William A Plapinger
David and Linda Pohs-Supino
John Porter Charitable Trust
Miss Victoria Provis
The Quercus Trust
Mr and Mrs J V Radford
Mr and Mrs P V Radford
Barbara Rae RA
John and Anne Raisman
Sir David and Lady Ramsbotham
Mrs Pauline Recanati
Mr T H Reitman
Sir John and Lady Riddell
The Roland Group of Companies Plc
Mr and Mrs Ian Rosenberg
Alastair and Sarah Ross Goobey
Mr and Mrs Kerry Rubie
The Audrey Sacher Charitable Trust
Dr P B St Leger
Mr and Mrs Victor Sandelson
Mr and Mrs Bryan Sanderson
Mr and Mrs Nicholas Sassow
Mrs Sylvia B Scheuer
Mr and Mrs Stuart L Scott
Dr Lewis Sevitt
The Countess of Shaftesbury
Mr and Mrs Paul Shang
Mr and Mrs Richard Sherrington
Mrs Lois Sieff OBE
Mr Peter Simon
Mr and Mrs John Sorrell
Don and Susan Starr
Mrs Jack Steinberg
Mr and Mrs David Stileman
John and Sheila Stoller
Mr and Mrs R W Strang
The Swan Trust
Mr and Mrs David Swift
Mr John Tackaberry
Mr and Mrs John D Taylor
Mrs Jonathan Todhunter
Mr and Mrs Julian Treger
Miss Joanna Trollope OBE
Carole Turner Record
Mrs Kathryn Uhde
Michael and Yvonne Uva
Mr and Mrs Tim Vignoles
Visa Lloyds Bank Monte Carlo
Mrs Catherine Vlasto
Mrs Claire Vyner
The Walter Guinness Charitable Trust
John B Watton
Mr and Mrs Jeffrey M Weingarten
Edna and Willard Weiss
Mrs Gerald Westbury
Mr Randall J Willette
Mr and Mrs Anthony Williams
Mr Jeremy Willoughby
Mr and Mrs Ami Wine
Mr John D Winter
Miss Caroline Wiseman
The Rt Hon Lord and Lady Young
of Graffham
and others who wish to remain anonymous

Schools Patrons Group
The Lord Aldington
Arts and Humanities Research Board
The Charlotte Bonham-Carter Charitable
Trust
Mrs Stephen Boyd
Mr Robert Bullock
The Candide Charitable Trust
Mr Raymond Cazalet
Smadar and David Cohen
Mr Simon Copsey
Keith and Pam Dawson
Debenhams Retail plc
The Delfont Foundation
The D'Oyly Carte Charitable Trust
Mr Alexander Duma
The Marchioness of Dufferin and Ava
The Gilbert & Eileen Edgar Foundation
The Eranda Foundation
Jack and Greta Goldhill
P H Holt Charitable Trust
The Lark Trust
Lora Lehmann
The Leverhulme Trust
The Loughborough Fellowship
in Fine Art
The Mercers' Company
The Henry Moore Foundation
Robin Heller Moss
The Mulberry Trust
Newby Trust Limited
N Peal Cashmere
The Worshipful Company of Painter-
Stainers
The Stanley Picker Trust
Pickett Fine Leather Ltd
Edith and Ferdinand Porjes Charitable
Trust
Rio Tinto plc
Mr and Mrs Anthony Salz
Paul Smith and Pauline Denyer Smith
The South Square Trust
Mr and Mrs Michele Sportelli
The Starr Foundation
The Steel Charitable Trust
Mr and Mrs Robert Lee Sterling Jr
The Peter Storrs Trust
Mr and Mrs Denis Tinsley
The Celia Walker Art Foundation
The Harold Hyam Wingate
Foundation
and others who wish to remain anonymous

General Benefactors
Mr Keith Bromley
Miss Jayne Edwardes
Catherine Lewis Foundation
Lady Sainsbury
The Schneer Foundation Inc
The Rt Hon Lord and Lady Young
of Graffham
and others who wish to remain anonymous

American Associates
Benefactors
American Express
Mrs Deborah Loeb Brice
Mr Francis Finlay
Mrs Melville Wakeman Hall
Mrs Jeanne K Lawrence
Sir Christopher and Lady Lewinton
Ms Brenda Neubauer Straus
WPP Group

Sponsors
Mrs Jan Cowles
Mrs Katherine D W Findlay
Mr Edward H Harte
Ms Frances S Hayward
Mr and Mrs Stephen M Kellen
Mr James Kemper Jr
The Honorable and Mrs Philip Lader
Mrs Linda Noe Laine
Mrs Edmond J Safra
Mr Peter Schoenfeld
Virgin Atlantic

Patrons
Ms Helen Harting Abell
Mr and Mrs Steven Ausnit
Mr and Mrs Stephen D Bechtel Jr
Mrs William J Benedict
Mr Donald A Best
Mr and Mrs Henry W Breyer III
Mrs Mildred C Brinn
Dr and Mrs Robert Carroll
Mr and Mrs Benjamin Coates
Ms Anne S Davidson
Ms Zita Davisson
Mr and Mrs Charles Diker
Mrs June Dyson
Mrs John W Embry
Mrs A Barlow Ferguson
Mrs Robert Ferst
Mr Richard E Ford
Mrs William Fox, Jr
Mr and Mrs Lawrence S Friedland
Goldman, Sachs & Co
Mrs Betty Gordon
Ms Rachel K Grody
Mr and Mrs Martin D Gruss
Mr and Mrs Gurnee F Hart
Mr and Mrs Gustave M Hauser
Mr and Mrs John R Hupper
Mr Robert J Irwin
Ms Betty Wold Johnson and Mr Douglas
Bushnell
The Honorable and Mrs W Eugene
Johnston III
Mr William W Karatz
Mr and Mrs Gary A Kraut
The Nathan Manilow Foundation
Mrs John P McGrath
Mrs Mark Millard
Mrs Barbara T Missett
Mr Paul D Myers
Mr and Mrs Wilson Nolen
Mrs Richard D O'Connor
Mr and Mrs Jeffrey Pettit
Mr Robert S Pirie
Mrs Virginia Ridder
Mrs Nanette Ross
Mrs Frances G Scaife
Ms Jan Blaustein Scholes
Mr and Mrs Stanley D Scott
Ms Georgia Shreve
Mr James Sollins
Mrs Frederick M Stafford
Mr and Mrs Stephen Stamas
Mr Arthur O Sulzberger and Ms Allison
S Cowles
Mrs Royce Deane Tate
Mrs Britt Tidelius
Ms Sue Erpf Van de Bovenkamp
Mrs Vincent S Villard, Jr
Mr and Mrs Stanford S Warshawsky
Mrs Sara E White
Dr and Mrs Robert D Wickham
Mr and Mrs Robert G Wilmers
Mr Robert W Wilson
Mr and Mrs Kenneth Woodcock
and others who wish to remain anonymous

Friends of the Royal Academy
Patron Friends
Mr Brian Bailey
Mrs Yvonne Barlow
Mr P F J Bennett
Mrs V Bondarenko
Mr and Mrs Sidney Corob
Mr David Duncan
Mr Michael Godbee
Ms Katrin Henkel
Mr S Isern-Feliu
Mr and Mrs S D Kahan
Mr David Ker
Mrs Joyce Lacerte
Mrs Maureen D Metcalfe
Mr R J Mullis
Mr and Mrs Derald H Ruttenberg
Mr Robin Symes
Mrs Cynthia H Walton
The Hon Mrs Simon Weinstock
and others who wish to remain anonymous

Supporting Friends
Ms Corinne Aldridge
Mr Richard B Allan
Mr Ian Anstruther
Mr Keith G Bennett
Mrs Susan Besser
Mrs C W T Blackwell
Mr C Boddington and Ms R Naylor
Mrs J M Bracegirdle
Mr Paul Brand
Mr Cornelius Broere
Mrs Anne Cadbury OBE JP DL
Miss E M Cassin
Mr R A Cernis
Mr S Chapman
Mr and Mrs John Cleese
Mr and Mrs Chris Cotton
Mrs M F Coward
Anthea Craigmyle
Mrs Nadine Crichton
Mr Julian R Darley
Mrs Belinda Davie
Mr John Denham
Miss N J Dhanani
Miss Carol Dodds
Mr Kenneth Edwards
Jack and Irene Finkler
Mrs Patricia Glasswell
Mrs R H Goddard
Mrs D Goodsell
Mr R Gow
Mr Gavin Graham
Mr and Mrs Jonathan Green
Mrs Richard Grogan
Miss Karen Harper-Gow
Mr Malcolm P Herring
Mr R J Hoare
Miss J Horsford
Mrs Manya Igel
Ms Shiblee Jamal
Mrs Jane Jason
Mrs G R Jeffries
Mr Roger A Jennings
Mr Harold Joels
Mr and Mrs J Kessler
Mrs L Kosta
Mrs Carol Kroch
Mrs Joan Lavender
Mr and Mrs David Leathers
Mr Owen Luder CBE PRIBA FRSA
Miss Julia MacRae
Mr Donald A Main
Lord Marks of Broughton
Mrs Janet Marsh
Mr J B H Martin
Mrs Gillian McIntosh
Mr R T Miles
Mrs A Morgan
Mrs Elizabeth M Newell
Miss Kim Nicholson
Mr Robert Linn Ottley
Mrs Anne Phillips
Mr Ralph Picken
Mr D B E Pike
Mr Ian Poynton
Mrs Beatrice Prevett
Mr Benjamin Pritchett-Brown
Mr W S C Richards OBE
Mrs Elizabeth Ridley
Mr F Peter Robinson
Mr D S Rocklin
Mrs A Rodman
Mr and Mrs O Roux
Dr Susan Saga
Lady Sainsbury
The Rt Hon Sir Timothy Sainsbury
Mrs E M Sandelson
Dr I B Schulenburg
Mrs D Scott
Mrs Josephine Seaton
Mrs E D Sellick
Mr and Mrs Richard Seymour
Mr R J Simmons CBE
Mr John H M Sims
Miss L M Slattery
Dr and Mrs M L Slotover
Mrs P Spanoghe
Professor Philip Stott
Mr James Stuart
Mrs J A Tapley
Mr W N Trotter
Mr and Mrs Ludovic de Walden
Miss J Waterous
Mrs Claire Weldon
Mr Frank S Wenstrom
Mrs Sheree D Whatley
Mrs Jacqueline Williams
Mr W M Wood
Mr R M Woodhouse
and others who wish to remain anonymous

CORPORATE MEMBERSHIP OF THE ROYAL ACADEMY OF ARTS
Launched in 1988, the Royal Academy's Corporate Membership Scheme has proved highly successful. With 104 members it is now the largest membership scheme in Europe.

Corporate membership offers company benefits to staff and clients and access to the Academy's facilities and resources. Each member pays an annual subscription to be a Member (£7,000) or Patron (£20,000).

Participating companies recognise the importance of promoting the visual arts. Their support is vital to the continuing success of the Academy.

Corporate Membership Scheme

Corporate Patrons

Andersen
Bloomberg LP
BNP Paribas
BP Amoco p.l.c.
Debenhams Retail plc
Deutsche Bank AG
The Economist Group
Ernst and Young
GlaxoSmithKline plc
Granada plc
John Lewis Partnership
Merrill Lynch
Radisson Edwardian Hotels
Royal & Sun Alliance

Honorary Corporate Patron

Credit Suisse First Boston

Corporate Members

Apax Partners Holding Ltd
Athenaeum Hotel
Aukett Europe
AXA UK plc
Bacon and Woodrow
Bank of America
Barclays plc
Bear, Stearns International Ltd
BG plc
BMP DDB Limited
Bonhams
The Boston Consulting Group
Bovis Lend Lease Limited
British Alcan Aluminium plc
The British Land Company PLC
BT plc
Bunzl plc
Cantor Fitzgerald
Cazenove & Co
CB Hillier Parker
Christie's
Chubb Insurance Company of Europe
CJA (Management Recruitment Consultants) Limited
Clayton Dubilier & Rice Limited
Clifford Chance
Colefax and Fowler Group
Cookson Group plc
Credit Agricole Indosuez
De Beers
Diageo plc
Dresdner Kleinwort Wasserstein
Eversheds
F&C Management plc
Gartmore Investment Management plc
Goldman Sachs International
Govett Investment Management Limited
H J Heinz Company Limited
HSBC plc
ICI
King Sturge
KPMG
Linklaters & Alliance
Macfarlanes
Man Group plc
McKinsey & Co.
M & C Saatchi
Morgan Stanley & Co International
MoMart Ltd
Newton Investment Management Ltd
Pearson plc
The Peninsular and Oriental Steam Navigation Company
Pentland Group plc
Provident Financial plc
Raytheon Systems Limited
Redwood
Reed Elsevier plc
Rowe & Maw
The Royal Bank of Scotland
Schroder Salomon Smith Barney
Schroders Investment Management Limited
Sea Containers Ltd.
SG
Six Continents PLC
Skanska Construction Group Limited
Slaughter and May
The Smith & Williamson Group
Sotheby's
Travelex
Trowers & Hamlins
Unilever UK Limited
UBS AG Private Banking

Honorary Corporate Members

All Nippon Airways Co. Ltd
A.T. Kearney Limited
Derwent Valley Holdings plc
London First
Reuters Limited
Yakult UK Limited

SPONSORS OF PAST EXHIBITIONS

The President and Council of the Royal Academy thank sponsors of past exhibitions for their support. Sponsors of major exhibitions during the last ten years have included the following:

Allied Trust Bank
Africa: The Art of a Continent, 1995*
Anglo American Corporation of South Africa
Africa: The Art of a Continent, 1995*
A.T. Kearney
231st Summer Exhibition, 1999
232nd Summer Exhibition, 2000
233rd Summer Exhibition, 2001
The Banque Indosuez Group
Pissarro: The Impressionist and the City, 1993
Barclays
Ingres to Matisse: Masterpieces of French Painting, 2001
BBC Radio One
The Pop Art Show, 1991
BMW (GB) Limited
Georges Rouault: The Early Years, 1903–1920. 1993
David Hockney: A Drawing Retrospective, 1995*
British Airways Plc
Africa: The Art of a Continent, 1995
BT
Hokusai, 1991
Cantor Fitzgerald
From Manet to Gauguin: Masterpieces from Swiss Private Collections, 1995
1900: Art at the Crossroads, 2000
The Capital Group Companies
Drawings from the J Paul Getty Museum, 1993
Chase Fleming Asset Management
The Scottish Colourists 1900–1930. 2000
Chilstone Garden Ornaments
The Palladian Revival: Lord Burlington and His House and Garden at Chiswick, 1995
Christie's
Frederic Leighton 1830–1896. 1996
Sensation: Young British Artists from The Saatchi Collection, 1997
Classic FM
Goya: Truth and Fantasy, The Small Paintings, 1994
The Glory of Venice: Art in the Eighteenth Century, 1994
Corporation of London
Living Bridges, 1996
Country Life
John Soane, Architect: Master of Space and Light, 1999
Credit Suisse First Boston
The Genius of Rome 1592–1623. 2000
The Daily Telegraph
American Art in the 20th Century, 1993
1900: Art at the Crossroads, 2000
De Beers
Africa: The Art of a Continent, 1995
Debenhams Retail plc
Premiums and RA Schools Show, 1999
Premiums and RA Schools Show, 2000
Premiums and RA Schools Show, 2001
Deutsche Morgan Grenfell
Africa: The Art of a Continent, 1995
Diageo plc
230th Summer Exhibition, 1998
The Drue Heinz Trust
The Palladian Revival: Lord Burlington and His House and Garden at Chiswick, 1995
Denys Lasdun, 1997
Tadao Ando: Master of Minimalism, 1998
The Dupont Company
American Art in the 20th Century, 1993
Elf
Alfred Sisley, 1992
Ernst & Young
Monet in the 20th Century, 1999
eyestorm
Apocalypse: Beauty and Horror in Contemporary Art, 2000
Fidelity Foundation
The Dawn of the Floating World (1650–1765). Early Ukiyo-e Treasures from the Museum of Fine Arts, Boston, 2001
Fondation Elf
Alfred Sisley, 1992
Friends of the Royal Academy
Victorian Fairy Painting, 1997
Game International Limited
Forty Years in Print: The Curwen Studio and Royal Academicians, 2001
The Jacqueline and Michael Gee Charitable Trust
LIFE? or THEATRE? The Work of Charlotte Salomon, 1999
Générale des Eaux Group
Living Bridges, 1996
Glaxo Wellcome plc
The Unknown Modigliani, 1994
Goldman Sachs International
Alberto Giacometti, 1901–1966. 1996
Picasso: Painter and Sculptor in Clay, 1998
The Guardian
The Unknown Modigliani, 1994
Guinness Peat Aviation
Alexander Calder, 1992
Guinness PLC (see Diageo plc)
223rd Summer Exhibition, 1991
224th Summer Exhibition, 1992
225th Summer Exhibition, 1993
226th Summer Exhibition, 1994
227th Summer Exhibition, 1995
228th Summer Exhibition, 1996
229th Summer Exhibition, 1997
Harpers & Queen
Georges Rouault: The Early Years, 1903–1920. 1993
Sandra Blow, 1994
David Hockney: A Drawing Retrospective, 1995*
Roger de Grey, 1996
The Headley Trust
Denys Lasdun, 1997
The Henry Moore Foundation
Alexander Calder, 1992
Africa: The Art of a Continent, 1995
Ibstock Building Products Ltd
John Soane, Architect: Master of Space and Light, 1999
The Independent
The Pop Art Show, 1991
Living Bridges, 1996
Apocalypse: Beauty and Horror in Contemporary Art, 2000
Industrial Bank of Japan, Limited
Hokusai, 1991
International Asset Management
Frank Auerbach, Paintings and Drawings 1954–2001. 2001
Donald and Jeanne Kahn
John Hoyland, 1999
Land Securities PLC
Denys Lasdun, 1997
The Mail on Sunday
Royal Academy Summer Season, 1992
Royal Academy Summer Season, 1993
Marks & Spencer
Royal Academy Schools Premiums, 1994
Royal Academy Schools Final Year Show, 1994*
Martini & Rossi Ltd
The Great Age of British Watercolours, 1750–1880. 1993
Paul Mellon KBE
The Great Age of British Watercolours, 1750–1880. 1993
Mercury Communications
The Pop Art Show, 1991
Merrill Lynch
American Art in the 20th Century, 1993*
Paris: Capital of the Arts 1900–1968. 2002
Midland Bank plc
RA Outreach Programme, 1992–1996
Lessons in Life, 1994
Minorco
Africa: The Art of a Continent, 1995
Natwest Group
Nicolas Poussin 1594–1665. 1995
The Nippon Foundation
Hiroshige: Images of Mist, Rain, Moon and Snow, 1997
Olivetti
Andrea Mantegna, 1992
Peterborough United Football Club
Art Treasures of England: The Regional Collections, 1997
Premiercare (National Westminster Insurance Services)
Roger de Grey, 1996*
RA Exhibition Patrons Group
Chagall: Love and the Stage, 1998
Kandinsky, 1999
Chardin 1699–1779. 2000
Botticelli's Dante: The Drawings for The Divine Comedy, 2001
Redab (UK) Ltd
Wisdom and Compassion: The Sacred Art of Tibet, 1992
Reed Elsevier plc
Van Dyck 1599–1641. 1999
Rembrandt's Women, 2001
Republic National Bank of New York
Sickert: Paintings, 1992
The Royal Bank of Scotland
Braque: The Late Works, 1997*
Premiums, 1997
Premiums, 1998
Premiums, 1999
Royal Academy Schools Final Year Show, 1996
Royal Academy Schools Final Year Show, 1997
Royal Academy Schools Final Year Show, 1998
The Sara Lee Foundation
Odilon Redon: Dreams and Visions, 1995
Sea Containers Ltd
The Glory of Venice: Art in the Eighteenth Century, 1994
Silhouette Eyewear
Wisdom and Compassion: The Sacred Art of Tibet, 1992
Sandra Blow, 1994
Africa: The Art of a Continent, 1995
Société Générale, UK
Gustave Caillebotte: The Unknown Impressionist, 1996*
Société Générale de Belgique
Impressionism to Symbolism: The Belgian Avant-Garde 1880–1900. 1994
Spero Communications
Royal Academy Schools Final Year Show, 1992
Thames Water Plc
Thames Water Habitable Bridge Competition, 1996
The Times
Wisdom and Compassion: The Sacred Art of Tibet, 1992
Drawings from the J Paul Getty Museum, 1993
Goya: Truth and Fantasy, The Small Paintings, 1994
Africa: The Art of a Continent, 1995
Time Out
Sensation: Young British Artists from The Saatchi Collection, 1997
Apocalypse: Beauty and Horror in Contemporary Art, 2000
Tractabel
Impressionism to Symbolism: The Belgian Avant-Garde 1880–1900, 1994
Union Minière
Impressionism to Symbolism: The Belgian Avant-Garde 1880–1900, 1994
Vistech International Ltd
Wisdom and Compassion: The Sacred Art of Tibet, 1992
Yakult UK Ltd
RA Outreach Programme, 1997–2000*
alive: Life Drawings from the Royal Academy of Arts & Yakult Outreach Programme

* Recipients of a Pairing Scheme Award, managed by Arts + Business. Arts + Business is funded by the Arts Council of England and the Department for Culture, Media and Sport.

OTHER SPONSORS

Sponsors of events, publications and other items in the past five years:

Carlisle Group plc
Country Life
Derwent Valley Holdings plc
Fidelity Foundation
Foster and Partners
Goldman Sachs International
Gome International
Rob van Helden
IBJ International plc
John Doyle Construction
Marks & Spencer
Michael Hopkins & Partners
Morgan Stanley Dean Witter
Prada
Radisson Edwardian Hotels
Richard and Ruth Rogers
Strutt & Parker